What They Didn't Teach You in **Russian** Class

Slang phrases for the café, club, bar, bedroom, ball game and more

Erin Coyne and Igor Fisun

 ULYSSES PRESS

To Myroslava.
Someday this book is gonna embarrass the hell out of you.

▲▼▲

Published by:
Ulysses Press
P.O. Box 3440
Berkeley, CA 94703
www.ulyssespress.com

ISBN: 978-1-61243-677-7
Library of Congress Control Number: 2016957905

Printed in the United States by Bang Printing
10 9 8 7 6 5 4

Acquisitions editor: Casie Vogel
Managing editor: Claire Chun
Editors: Shayna Keyles, Alice Riegert
Proofreader: Renee Rutledge
Design and layout: what!design @ whatweb.com
Illustrations: what!design @ whatweb.com

Table of Contents

Using This Book

US–Soviet...er, Russian relations have never been stranger. And not only have the politics changed, but some of the language Russians use has changed, too. Thus, we offer you *What They Didn't Teach You in Russian Class* as a sort of follow-up to the previously published *Dirty Russian*.

Russian is just about the coolest language in the world. But you already know that, because you've been studying the language for a while now, right? This book wasn't written with the novice in mind—but don't worry, beginners, I've included pronunciation tips and a few grammar refreshers for you. The book is designed to bring your Russian to the next level, a level usually reserved for natives and longtime expats. With that in mind, I've tried to give you all the dirty words and insider terms that your college Russian professor would never teach you. So you're not gonna find any basic vocabulary or grammar lessons or phrases for asking where the library is. But if you're looking to tell somebody to fuck off or score a hot Russian date, then you're in the right place, my friend.

All of this is to say that I hope you already more or less understand the language before jumping into this book.

Russian is a complex language to master even at a fairly basic level. Learning the slang is even harder, as it can be extremely difficult for the uninitiated to gauge when, where, and with whom slang is appropriate. As the old saying goes: When in doubt, leave it out. Using the wrong slang or profanity with the wrong person at the wrong time—especially with a strong foreign accent—will make you sound ridiculous, at best. So err on the side of caution. Also, be aware that in Russia, it is far less socially acceptable for women to use foul language, so know your audience before letting it rip.

Some things haven't changed that much since *Dirty Russian* came out, so you'll still find all the classic insults and expletives that were covered the first time around. Now, before you start clutching your pearls and sputtering, "But, but, but...it's so *vulgar*," you can relax. Yes, vulgarity is a part of language. That's not to say that you should open your dirty mouth and let it loose, but you should be aware of some of these more "colorful" terms, because there's a good chance you may hear them. Still, you should definitely use your head before using some of these words and phrases yourself. If you use vulgarity indiscriminately, you will likely amuse at best and offend at worst. But as long as you're with some chill friends with a sense of humor, you should be good to go, especially if the alcohol is flowing.

We have tried to make the book as reader-friendly as possible. Each phrase in the book is accompanied by its English equivalent and its Russian pronunciation. Often, you'll find example sentences with key terms bolded so you can break those words out and employ them on your own, whether you're just joking around with your friends at school or spending quality time on the streets of Moscow, St. Petersburg, Kiev, or some remote backwater village. Once you start to know your way around and find yourself with a group of sailor-mouthed friends with three days' worth of drinkin' on their breath, you should jump right in and start throwing the slang around. Even clumsy attempts will likely earn their amused affection.

We hope this doesn't come as news to you, but right now, Russia is relevant! I mean, we always knew it was important, but it's gotten a lot more in-your-face lately, thanks to shifting political alliances and agendas. In light of current events, there is now a section called "Putin Is a Dickhead," which I guess means my Russian visa application won't be approved any time soon. The computer slang called язык падонков (*yazik padonkov*) has mostly died its well-deserved death (honestly, it was annoying as hell!), and has been replaced by the world of mobile apps and selfie sticks. Most depressing of all, American fast food chains continue their nefarious spread through the streets and stomachs of Russia, so if you want to order some chicken poppers at Papa John's or a caramel frappuccino at Starbucks, we now have you covered.

For now, just sit back, crack open the book, and tell everyone around you to fuck the hell off. Now let's get some of the basics over with so we can move on to the good stuff.

Some basics

Russian, much like Russia itself, is not for the faint of heart. So here are a few notes to keep in mind as you're reading.

Ty and Vy: Like many languages, Russian has two pronouns for "you": ты/*ty* and вы/*vy*. *Ty* is the informal and singular way of saying "you"; *vy* is formal and plural. We have used *ty* as the default in this book, as many of the terms within are inherently linked to informal social situations. Generally, you wouldn't say anything in this book to someone that you are on *vy* terms with. *Vy*, however, is also used for plurals, so this is the one you need when talking to more than one person.

Cases: Russian has six grammatical cases, which means that the endings of words change depending on their function in the sentence (direct object, indirect object, object of a preposition, etc.). When words are given in isolation, assume that they are in the nominative case. However, when they are given in phrases, they have whatever case ending is necessary for the grammatical context. As this is not a first-year Russian textbook, familiarity of basic Russian grammar is presumed. If none of this paragraph made sense to you, go look it up.

Gender: All Russian nouns have a gender (masculine, feminine, or neuter). This is important, because gender will affect declensional patterns as well as the endings you use on adjectives to describe nouns. When discussing people, gender means that both adjectives and the past tense of verbs take different endings depending on whether you are talking about a man or a woman. In most cases, we have used masculine endings as a sort of "default" gender. Feminine endings are used only when specified as such. If that seems sexist to anyone, well, what can I say? That's Russia—you might as well get used to it now.

Pronunciation: The most important thing when it comes to pronunciation in Russian is stress. Once you find the correct stressed syllable in a word, the rest of the pronunciation should fall into place. In this book, stress is indicated in the transliteration line by capital letters. There are some finer points of pronunciation that aren't as essential, such as voicing and devoicing. If you screw those up, you'll sound totally foreign, but you'll still be understood.

Slang
slyeng
Сленг

Here are some relevant terms before we begin:

Jargon
zhar-GON
Жаргон
Another term that basically means "slang," but most often used when talking about criminal slang.

Cussing
ru-GA-tyel-stvo
Ругательство

Obscene language
mat
Мат

To curse using obscene language
ma-tye-RIT-sya
Материться

Indecent language
nye-nor-ma-TIV-na-ya LYEK-si-ka
Ненормативная лексика

Pronouncing Russian

Here's the Russian alphabet. Most of it isn't too tricky, but there are few sounds that differ from English.

Аа sounds like "ah," as in "open your mouth and say 'ah.'"

Бб sounds like "b." At the end of a word, it sounds like "p."

Вв sounds like "v." At the end of a word, it sounds like "f."

Гг sounds like "g." At the end of a word, it is pronounced "k."

Дд sounds like "d." At the end of a word, it is pronounced "t."

Ее sounds like "yeh." If unstressed, it usually sounds more like "ee."

Ёё sounds like "yo," as in "Yo!" This letter can only appear in stressed positions, so if a word changes stress when put into a different case, this letter falls out and becomes a regular ol' "e."

Жж sounds like "zh," like the *g* in "massage." This consonant is always hard; at the end of a word, it sounds like "sh."

Зз sounds like "z." At the end of a word, it is pronounced "s."

Ии sounds like "ee," as in "Eeek!"

Йй sounds like "y," sort of like the *y* in "day."

Кк sounds like "k."

Лл sounds like "l."

Мм sounds like "m."

Нн sounds like "n."

Оо sounds like "o," as in "folk." If unstressed, it is pronounced like an "a."

Пп sounds like "p."

Рр sounds like "r." This is trilled.

Сс sounds like "s."

Тт sounds like "t."

Уу sounds like "oo," as in "boot."

Фф sounds like "f."

Хх sounds like "kh," sort of like the *ch* in "achtung."

Цц sounds like "ts." This consonant is always hard.

Чч sounds like "ch." This consonant is always soft.

Шш sounds like "sh." This consonant is always hard.

Щщ sounds like "sch," like "fresh chicken." This consonant is always soft.

ъ is a hard sign. This causes the preceding consonant to harden.

ы sounds like saying "it" and "eat" at the same time. If you can do that, then you'll be pretty close. If you can't do that, err on the side of *i* in "it."

ь is a soft sign. This softens the preceding consonant.

Ээ sounds like "eh."

Юю sounds like "yu."

Яя sounds like "ya." If unstressed, it usually sounds closer to "ee."

Some combined sounds:

ай sounds like "ay," as in "Ay, carumba!"

ой sounds like "oy," as in "boy." If unstressed, it's "ay."

ей sounds like "ei," as in "weight."

дж sounds like "j," as in "Joe."

CHAPTER 1

Meet & Greet

VSTRYE-cha i pri-VYET-stvi-ye

Встреча и Приветствие

Greetings in Russia are pretty much like greetings everywhere else: There's some version of "Hello," "How are you?" etc. There's no real trick, except that you need to remember who you're talking to. If you're talking to someone you don't know very well who's over the age of, say, 30, stick with the formal *vy*. With younger people, you can pretty safely use the informal *ty*, especially if you are in a chill social situation among friends. Keep in mind that using *ty* with the wrong person in Russia is a pretty serious insult that will piss some people off.

Howdy!

ZDRA-sstye!

Здрассте!

Saying hello seems simple enough, right? Well, it is, but if you're a guy and don't shake on it, you'll be considered a total asshole. If you're a chick and *do* shake hands, they'll think you're, well, foreign, and a little weird. And if you're greeting someone you know fairly well, there'll be kissing involved, whether you like it or not. Russians generally have a very different concept of personal space than Americans do, so just suck it up, say your hellos, and move on.

Hi!
pri-VYET!
Привет!

Hiya!
pri-VYET-iki!
Приветики!
Kinda cutesy, most often used informally among friends.

Sup, guys!
zdo-RO-vo, re-BYA-ta!
Здорово, ребята!
Remember to watch your stress with this word. The greeting is *zdo-RO-vo*. With the stress *ZDO-ro-vo*, it means something more like "awesome."

What's up?
kak de-LA?
Как дела?

How ya doin'?
kak ti?
Как ты?

What's new?
chto NO-vo-go?
Что нового?

How's life?
kak zhi-VYOSH?
Как живёшь?

What's the word?
chto SLISH-no?
Что слышно?

What's happenin'?
chto strya-SLOS?
Что стряслось?

Hey, honey, **what's up?**
pri-VYET, kra-SOT-ka, kak del-ISH-ki?
Привет, красотка, как **делишки**?
Kinda cutesy.

....

Everything's just hunky-dory
vsyo i-DYOT kak po MA-slu
Всё идёт как по маслу

When I talk to Russians who have been to the United States, the one thing that they all say annoys the crap out of them is the insincerity of the American "How are you?" greeting. It's because that question is always answered with a big, stupid grin and an "I'm fine," no matter how obvious it is that the person is in a shitty, pissed-off mood. So when Russians ask you how you are, go ahead and tell them the truth. They asked for it.

It's all good!
vsyo kho-ro-SHO!
Всё хорошо!

Everything's okay.
vsyo o-KEI.
Всё о-кей.

Fine.
nor-MAL-no.
Нормально.

Chill.
nor-MUL.
Нормуль.

Peachy.
CHU-denko.
Чудненько.

Okey-dokey.
LA-den-ko.
Ладненько.

Everything's all right.
u me-NYA vsyo v po-RYAD-kye.
У меня всё в порядке.

Fuckin' cool!
o-KHU-enno!
Охуенно!

Couldn't be better!
LU-chshe vsyekh!
Лучше всех!

Pretty fuckin' good!
pi-ZDA-to!
Пиздато!

Fucking awesome!
za-ye-BIS!
Заебись!
The word can either mean "really good" or "really fucking awful," depending on how you use it.

I'm fresh as a daisy.
ya SVYE-zhii kak o-GUR-chik.
Я свежий как огурчик.
Literally, "fresh as a cucumber." This is usually said by someone in denial about how shitfaced they are.

No worries.
vsyo po ti-KHON-ku.
Всё по тихоньку.

Same old, same old.
vsyo po STA-romu.
Всё по старому.

Why do you give a fuck?
tye-BYA E-to ye-BYOT, chto li?
Тебя это ебёт, что ли?

Don't even ask!
nye SPRA-shi-vai!
Не спрашивай!

A complete mess!
POL-nii ab-ZATS!
Полный абзац!

Pretty crappy.
khren-O-vo.
Хреново.

Really shitty.
khu-yO-vo.
Хуёво.

I'm in a crappy mood.
ya v kher-O-vom na-stro-yE-ni-ye.
Я в херовом настроении.

I must have gotten up on the wrong side of the bed today.
ya na-VYER-no se-VOD-nya vstal s LYE-voi no-GI.
Я наверное сегодня встал с левой ноги.
Or sometimes не с той ноги (*nye s TOI no-GI*).

My life has turned into a **total nightmare**.
mo-YA zhizn pre-vra-TI-las v splosh-NOI kosh-MAR.
Моя жизнь превратилась **в сплошной кошмар**.

Really sucky.
POL-na-ya ZHO-pa.
Полная жопа.
Literally, "total ass."

Fucking awful!
ya v piz-DYE!
Я в пизде!
Literally, "I'm in the pussy."

Totally fucked up!
POL-nii piz-DYETS!
Полный пиздец!
If you want to soften this phrase up a bit, you can use the words пипец (*pi-PYETZ*) and копец (*ka-PYETS*), which are both sort of euphemistic forms of the word пиздец.

That's the deal.
vot ta-KI-ye pi-rozh-KI.
Вот такие пирожки.
Usually said after a detailed explanation of what has happened to you recently.

....

Hell if I know
chort ye-VO ZNA-yet
Чёрт его знает

There are only 24 hours in a day, so there's just no way that you can be expected to know everything about everything.

I don't know.
ya nye ZNA-yu.
Я не знаю.

I'm out of the loop.
ya nye v KUR-sye.
Я не в курсе.

This is the first I've heard of it.
PYER-vii raz SLI-shu.
Первый раз слышу.

I have no idea.
po-NYA-ti-ya ne I-me-yu.
Понятия не имею.

Time will tell.
po-zhi-VYOM, u-VI-dim.
Поживём, увидим.

What's that thingy?
chto E-to za khren-o-TYEN?
Что это за **хренотень**?

God only knows.
bog ye-VO ZNA-yet.
Бог его знает.

Fuck if I know.
khui ye-VO ZNA-yet.
Хуй его знает.

There's just no understanding Russia.
u-mOm ro-SSI-yu nye po-NYAT.
Умом Россию не понять.
You can usually score some cultural points with this famous line from a
poem by Fyodor Tyutchev.

....

Let's be friends!
BU-dyem dru-ZYA-mi!
Будем друзьями!

In America, we tend to be polite to strangers but treat our
friends like shit because, hey, they'll forgive us. Russians
are sort of the opposite: They tend to be total assholes

to strangers but are fiercely loyal and embarrassingly generous to those they consider part of their inner circle. So here are a few phrases to help you break the ice with your new Russian acquaintances, and maybe make yourself an ally in the process.

Let's use *ty*.
da-VAI na ti.
Давай на ты.
Once you start getting to know someone better, this is the way that you suggest taking the next step and moving to the informal "you."

Could you show me around the city?
ti bi nye mog mnye GO-rod po-ka-ZAT?
Ты бы не мог мне город показать?

You wanna come over to my place?
KHO-chesh ko mnye v GO-sti?
Хочешь ко мне в гости?

Let's chat!
da-VAI po-bol-TA-yem!
Давай поболтаем!

Let's hang out a bit.
da-VAI po-ob-SCHA-yem-sya.
Давай пообщаемся.

I feel like shooting the shit with someone.
KHO-chet-sya s kyem-to po-piz-DYET.
Хочется с кем-то **попиздеть**.

I want to chew the fat with someone.
kho-CHU s kyem-to po-trye-PA-tsya!
Хочу с кем-то **потрепаться**.

I hope I'll find some common ground with them.
na-DYE-yus, nai-DU s NI-mi O-bschii ya-ZIK.
Надеюсь, найду с ними **общий язык**.

I don't know anyone here, but I'd like to **meet some cool folks.**
ya ni-ko-VO ne ZNA-yu tut, no kho-TYEL-os bi po-znaKO-mit-sya s KLA-ssni-mi re-BYA-ta-mi.
Я никого не знаю тут, но хотелось бы **познакомиться с классными ребятами**.

....

Long time no see!
SKOL-ko lyet SKOl-ko zim!
Сколько лет сколько зим!

I don't get around as much as I used to, so when I do hit the town, it is always nice to run into an old pal. When a familiar face appears, go ahead and tell them how nice it is to see them.

Who do I see there!
ko-VO ya VI-zhu!
Кого я вижу!

Where have you been?
ku-DA ti pro-PAL?
Куда ты пропал?

Fancy meeting you here!
ka-KI-mi sud-BA-mi?
Какими судьбами?

Speak of the devil!
LYO-gok na po-MI-nye!
Лёгок на помине!

Hey, old man, **good to see you!**
eh, sta-rRIK, rad te-BYA VI-dyet!
Эй, старик, **рад тебя видеть**!

I've missed you!
ya po te-BYE so-SKU-chil-sya!
Я по тебе соскучился!

Please and thank you
po-ZHA-lui-sta i spa-SI-bo
Пожалуйста и спасибо

If you've studied any Russian at all, then you know that one of the funny things about the language is that "please" and "you're welcome" are the same word: пожалуйста (*po-ZHAL-uis-ta*). This can start to sound a little lame after a while: пожалуйста, спасибо (*spa-SI-bo*), пожалуйста, спасибо, on and on and on and on. So if you want to avoid sounding like a broken record, here are a few phrases you can use to add a little variety into the mix.

I have a **favor** to ask you.
u me-NYA k te-BYE PRO-sba.
У меня к тебе **просьба**.

Be a pal!
bud DRU-gom!
Будь другом!

Help me out!
bud lyu-BYE-zen!
Будь любезен!

I'm really asking you!
ya te-BYA O-chen prosh-U!
Я тебя очень прошу!

I'm begging you!
ya te-BYA u-mo-LYA-yu!
Я тебя умоляю!

I'm very grateful.
ya O-chen bla-go-DA-ren.
Я очень благодарен.
This is pretty formal and official sounding.

I thank you.
bla-go-dar-IU.
Благодарю.
This is also formal, but is sometimes used ironically by young people.

Thanks!
spa-SI-boch-ki!
Спасибочки!
Kind of a cutesy way of saying thanks.

....

No problem!
byez pro-BLYEM!
Без проблем!

If you're friends with a Russian, it's taken for granted that you'll be willing to lend a hand when needed, without complaint, and without too many questions. Here are few ways to tell your Russian pal that you're cool with that.

Don't worry about it!
da LAD-no!
Да ладно!

Don't mention it.
NYE za chto.
Не за что.
Be careful with stress. To say "Don't mention it," you have to stress it *NYE za chto*. If you say *nye za CHTO*, it means something like "No way, no how."

No biggie!
da E-to fig-NYA!
Да это фигня!

It's nothing!
nye STO-it!
Не стоит!
Yet another place where stress is important. Here you need *nye STO-it.* If you say *nye sto-IT,* you'll be saying "It doesn't stand."

Piece of cake!
ZA-pro-sto!
Запросто!

Nothin' to it!
NYE fig DYE-lat!
Не фиг делать!

Enjoy it (in health)!
na zdo-RO-vye!
На здоровье!

My bad!
iz-vi-NYA-yus!
Извиняюсь!

Sooner or later, you're going to make an ass of yourself. You just are. So here are few ways to say a quick apology and shake it off.

Excuse me!
iz-vi-NI!
Извини!

I'm sorry!
pro-STI!
Прости!

Whoops!
O-pa!
Опа!

SURPRISE
U-DI-VLYE-NI-YE
УДИВЛЕНИЕ

Life in Russia is full of surprises, which might be why Russians have so many words and expressions that essentially all mean "wow."

Wow!	*vau!*	Вау!
Wowzers!	*ukh, ti!*	Ух, ты!
My word!	*ye-SCHO bi!*	Ещё бы!
Well, how'd ya like that!	*nu, ti da-YOSH!*	Ну, ты даёшь!
Well, dang!	*o-bal-DYET!*	Обалдеть!
That's wild!	*o-fi-GYET!*	Офигеть!
I'll be damned!	*o-du-RYET!*	Одуреть!
Holy shit!	*o-khu-YET!*	Охуеть!
Fuckin' A!	*za-ye-BIS!*	Заебись!
That's fucked up!	*E-ta piz-DYETZ!*	Это пиздец!
Fuck!	*yob!*	Ёб!
Eh, not bad!	*ni-che-VO se-BYE!*	Ничего себе!
Holy cow!	*ni fig-A se-BYE!*	Ни фига себе!
Gosh!	*ni khren-A se-BYE!*	Ни хрена себе!
Fuck yeah!	*ni khu-YA se-BYE!*	Ни хуя себе!

These last four are also often used sarcastically; for example, when you think someone has acted really out of line and you say to yourself, "You gotta be kiddin' me."

Sorry!
SO-ri!
Сори!
It's just like English, only with a Russian *o* and a rolled *r*.

For God's sake, forgive me!
pro-STI me-NYA, RA-di BO-ga!
Прости меня, ради Бога!

I was just kidding.
ya po-shu-TIL.
Я пошутил.

I don't know what's wrong with me.
ya nye ZNA-yu, chto so mnoi.
Я не знаю, что со мной.

I'm such an idiot.
VOT ya i-di-OT.
Вот я идиот!

It's all my fault.
ya vo vsyom vi-no-VAT.
Я во всём виноват.

Don't be upset with me!
nye o-bi-ZHAI-sya!
Не обижайся!

Don't hold a grudge.
zla na mye-NYA nye dyer-ZHI.
Зла на меня не держи.

I frickin' swear, I didn't do it on purpose!
BLYA BU-du, ya nye spye-tsi-AL-no!
Бля буду, я не специально!

I'm off!
ya po-SHOL!
Я пошёл!

Russians aren't known for being in a hurry, so parties, casual meetings, and chance encounters can become long, drawn out, and downright tiresome. Here are a few verbal cues to let your friends know that you're ready to make a getaway.

Bye!
po-KA!
Пока!

See ya later!
do VSTRYE-chi!
До встречи!

See ya soon!
do SKO-ro-vo!
До скорого!

Don't be a stranger!
ne pro-pa-DAI!
Не пропадай!

It's time for us (to go)!
nam po-RA!
Нам пора!

Let's roll!
AI-da!
айда!

Let's fucking bail already!
po-PIZ-di-li u-ZHE!
Попиздили уже!

It's time for me to **get the fuck outta** here.
mnye po-RA sye-BAT-sya.
Мне пора **съебаться**.

It's getting kinda late.
u-ZHE ne-DYET-sko-ye VRYE-mya.
Уже недетское время.

I'll call you.
ya te-BYE po-zvo-NIU.
Я тебе позвоню.

Hey, you!
eh, ti!
Эй, ты!

Sometimes, you just want to give a shout out to someone you see on the street. Here are ways to get their attention.

Hey...!
eh...!
Эй...!

little girl
DYE-voch-ka
девочка
This is generally used for a girl up to about age 12 or so.

little boy
mal-CHISH-ka
мальчишка

young man
mo-lo-DOI che-lo-VYEK
молодой человек
This can be used for any guy up to about age 30.

miss
DYE-vu-shka
девушка
This is for females up to about age 30.

ma'am
ZHEN-schi-na
женщина
For women over 30 or so.

lady
BA-rish-nya
барышня

grandma
BA-bu-shka
бабушка
For old ladies; just try to resist the American urge to say *ba-BU-shka*. It's *BA-bu-shka*, dammit.

granny
ba-BU-lya
бабуля
Also for old ladies, but probably somewhat more common in small towns and villages.

gramps
dye-DU-lya
дедуля

old man
sta-RIK
старик

pal
pri-YA-tyel
приятель

buddy
dru-ZHOK
дружок

guys
re-BYA-ta
ребята

bro
bra-TAN
братан

dude
chu-VAK
чувак

comrade
to-VA-risch
товарищ
Mainly used by old communists and ironic young people.

citizen
gra-zhda-NIN
гражданин
This is pretty Soviet sounding, but still occasionally used.

Russian doesn't make very wide use of titles. When Russians want to address someone formally, they use the name and patronymic formula (you know, like Иван Иванович, or Ivan Ivanovich) instead of something like Mister or Miss. When titles are used, it is mainly with foreigners who expect that sort of thing. Also, most foreign names don't lend themselves well to Russification and end up sounding pretty silly when you try. So for those occasions, use these terms.

Mister
go-spo-DIN
Господин

Miss
go-spo-ZHA
Госпожа

In formal public speeches, you may also sometimes hear:

Ladies and gentlemen!
DA-mi i go-spo-DA!
Дамы и господа!

CHAPTER 2

Friends & Enemies

dru-ZYA i vra-GI

Друзья и Враги

In the US, we tend to call just about everyone we know our "friends." Russians are not nearly so casual about relationships, however. To them, a friend is someone who has been through thick and thin with you, someone who would share his last beer with you and bail you out of jail. For all those other people that you just hang out with, there are different words to describe the more casual nature of your relationship.

Friends

dru-ZYA

Друзья

You're a **good friend** (male/female).
ti kho-RO-shii drug/kho-RO-sha-ya po-DRU-ga.
Ты **хороший друг/хорошая подруга**.

He is my very **best friend** in the world.
on moi SA-mii LU-chshii drug v MI-rye.
Он мой самый **лучший друг** в мире.

Me and my **buddies** usually go shoot the shit after work.
mi so svo-I-mi pri-YA-tel-ya-mi o-BI-chno vstre-CHA-yem-sya,
CHTO-by popi-ZDYET PO-sle ra-BO-ti.
Мы со своими **приятелями** обычно встречаемся, что-бы попиздеть после работы.

Hey, **guys**, let's party!
eh, pa-tsa-NI, da-VAi po-tu-SU-yem-sya!
Эй, **пацаны**, давай потусуемся!

Dudes, let's go for a beer.
mu-zhi-KI, poi-DYOM za PI-vom.
Мужики, пойдём за пивом.

He's my **(college) classmate** at the uni.
on moi od-no-KURS-nik v u-ni-VER-ye.
Он мой **однокурсник** в универе.

We're **roommates** in the dorm.
mi so-SYE-di po KO-mna-tye v ob-SCHA-gye.
Мы **соседи по комнате** в общаге.

Acquaintances, coworkers, and enemies
zna-KO-mi-ye, so-TRUD-ni-ki, i vra-GI
Знакомые, сотрудники, и враги

What's that **chick's** name?
kak E-tu dev-CHON-ku zo-VUT?
Как эту **девчонку** зовут?

All **broads** are wenches.
vsye BA-bi—STYER-vi.
Все **бабы**—стервы.
This is actually the name of a Russian pop song.

This **acquaintance** of mine once hitchhiked from Moscow to Irkutsk.

*o-DIN moi **zna-KO-mii** od-NA-zhdi YE-khal av-to-STOPom ot mosk-VI do ir-KUTSK-a.*

Один мой **знакомый** однажды ехал автостопом от Москвы до Иркутска.

I never give my phone number to **strangers**.

*ya ni-kog-DA nye da-YU svoi NO-mer te-le-FO-na **nezna-KOM-tsam**.*

Я никогда не даю свой номер телефона **незнакомцам**.

My **colleagues** and I are here on a business trip.

*mi so svo-I-mi **ko-LLYE-ga-mi** zdyes v ko-mman-dir-Ovkye.*

Мы со своими **коллегами** здесь в командировке.

Their **CEO** was arrested last week for fraud.

*ikh **GYE-na** byl a-res-TO-van na PRO-shloi ne-DYE-lye za mo-SHEN-i-chest-vo.*

Их **гена** был арестован на прошлой неделе за мошенничество.

My boss pays me **under the table**.

*moi shef mnye **PLA-tit v kon-VYER-tye**.*

Мой шеф мне платит **в конверте**.

My **manager** is sleeping with his secretary.

*moi **MA-na-ger** spit so svo-YEI se-kre-TAR-shei.*

Мой **манагер** спит со своей секретаршей.

This is the slangy pronunciation of менеджер (*ME-ne-dzher*).

Boris is my **mortal enemy**.

*bo-RIS—moi **za-KLYA-tii vrag**.*

Борис—мой **заклятый враг**.

I hate that **jerk**!

*ya ne-na-VI-zhu E-tu **tvar**!*

Я ненавижу эту **тварь**!

Literally, this means a beast, like an uncivilized animal.

Alexei is a **fucking idiot.**
*a-le-XEI – **dol-bo-YOB***
Алексей – **долбоёб**.

....

Compliments
kom-pli-MYEN-ti
Комплименты

Even the gruffest of Russians can often be won over with
a few kind words; however, they tend to be very sensitive
to insincerity. So if you want to compliment a Russian, you
better keep it real. Or better yet, follow it up with alcohol
and chocolate.

You rock!
ti PRO-sto mo-lo-DYETS!
Ты просто молодец!
Molodyets is sort of an all-purpose compliment that can mean anything
from "Good job" to "You're a swell guy."

Clever!
ti UM-nich-ka!
Ты умничка!

That's a hell of an idea!
E-to SU-per-ska-ya i-DYE-ya!
Это суперская идея!

That's brilliant!
E-to ge-ni-AL-na-ya misl!
Это гениальная мысль!

Cool threads!
KLASS-ni-ye SHMOT-ki!
Классные шмотки!

I really dig...
ya PRO-sto bal-DYE-yu ot...
Я просто балдею от...
Note that this phrase is followed by the genitive case.

> your **retro** style.
> *tvo-ye-VO **KLYO-vo-vo** STIL-ya.*
> твоего **клёвого** стиля.

> your **rad** hairstyle.
> *tvo-YEI **o-bal-DYE-nnoi** pri-CHO-ski.*
> твоей **обалденной** причёски.

> your **fashionable** jeans.
> *tvo-IKH **MOD-nikh** JINS-ov.*
> твоих **модных** джинсов.

> your **hip** (eye)glasses.
> *tvo-IKH **pri-KOL-nikh** och-KOV.*
> твоих **прикольных** очков.

You have awesome taste.
*u te-BYA **o-fig-YE-nnii** vkus.*
У тебя **офигенный** вкус.

You look really cool.
*ti **KLASS-no** VI-glyad-ish.*
Ты **классно** выглядишь.

You look great in that dress.
*ti **KRU-to** VI-glyad-ish v E-tom PLA-tye.*
Ты **круто** выглядишь в этом платье.

He's a real card.
*on ta-KOI **u-GAR-nii.***
Он такой **угарный.**

She's a really cool girl.
*on-A **KLASS-na-ya** dyev-CHON-ka.*
Она **классная** девчонка.

He's an **awesome guy.**
on SLAV-nii PAR-en.
Он **славный парень**.

She's such a **sweetheart.**
o-NA ta-KA-ya NYASH-na-ya.
Она такая **няшная**.

I envy you.
ya te-BYE za-VID-u-yu.
Я тебе завидую.

In Russian, there are two kinds of envy: белая зависть (*BYELa-ya ZA-vist*), or "white envy," and чёрная зависть (*CHORNa-ya ZA-vist*), or "black envy." White envy is the good kind, where ultimately you are genuinely happy for the person and their good fortune. Black envy is the kind where you secretly wish the person would spontaneously combust right in front of you so that you could witness their suffering and death, and then confiscate the object of your envy so that it can be yours, all yours!

Cool!
KLASS-no!
Классно!

Klassno is still the most common way of saying "Cool!" It is also often shortened to класс (*klass*). Here are few others:

Rad!
a-TAS-no!
Атасно!

Groovy!
KLYO-vo!
Клёво!

That's hilarious!
pri-KOL-no!
Прикольно!

Super!
SU-per!
Супер!

Now you're talkin'!
vot E-to da!
Вот это да!

....

Time for a little romance
po-RA dlya ro-MAN-ti-ki
Пора для романтики

Those long Russian nights can get a little lonely, so why not find someone who'll make the time fly by? Keep in mind that dating in Russia is a bit like dating during the Eisenhower years, but with more sex. Guys generally make all the moves and are expected to foot the bill. They're also expected to hold open doors, help put on coats, and offer a hand to assist their female companions out of cars—so be prepared to work if you're looking for a payoff. Oh, and if you decide to bring your girl flowers, make sure you buy an odd number—even-numbered bouquets are only for funerals, and that's probably not quite the message you want to send before an evening of romance.

To flirt
flirt-o-VAT
Флиртовать

I am really sick of guys **always hitting on me** at parties.
*mnye na-do-YElo, kak PAR-ni po-sto-YA-nno **pri-sta-YUT ko mnye** na vecher-IN-kakh.*
Мне надоело, как парни постоянно **пристают ко мне** на вечеринках.

Where can I **pick up** a chick/guy around here?
gdye tut MO-zhno snyat TYOL-ku/PAR-nya?
Где тут можно **снять** тёлку/парня?

Could I get your number?
MO-zhno tvoi te-le-FON-chik?
Можно твой телефончик?

What's your sign?
kto ti po zo-di-A-ku?
Кто ты по зодиаку?

Do you believe in **love at first sight?**
ti VYER-ish v lyu-BOV s PYER-vo-vo VZGLYA-da?
Ты веришь в **любовь с первого взгляда**?

I think we've met somewhere before.
po-MO-ye-mu, mi GDYE-to u-ZHE vstre-CHAL-is.
По-моему, мы где-то уже встречались.

I am mad about you!
ya skho-ZHU po tye-BYE s u-MA!
Я схожу по тебе с ума!

Can I buy you a drink?
MO-zhno te-BYA u-go-STIT chem-ni-BUD VI-pit?
Можно тебя угостить чем-нибудь выпить?

My friend thinks you're really cute.
moi drug schi-TA-yet te-BYA O-chen sim-pa-TICH-noi.
Мой друг считает тебя очень симпатичной.

Hey, **beautiful**, wanna get to know each other better?
pri-VYET, kra-SA-vi-tsa, KHO-chesh po-zna-KOM-it-sya po-BLI-zhe?
Привет, **красавица**, хочешь познакомиться поближе?
This is the feminine form. You could call a guy красавчик (*kra-SAV-chik*).

TERMS OF ENDEARMENT
LAS-KO-VI-YE SLO-VA
ЛАСКОВЫЕ СЛОВА

Dear (male/female)
do-ro-GOI/do-ro-GA-ya
Дорогой/дорогая

Dearie
do-ro-GU-sha
Дорогуша

My darling (male/female)
moi MI-len-kii/mo-YA MI-len-ka-ya
Мой миленький/моя миленькая

My better half
mo-YA LUCH-sha-ya po-lo-VIN-ka
Моя лучшая половинка

My sweetie pie
moi PUP-sik
Мой пупсик

My sweetie (male/female)
moi lyu-BIM-chik/mo-YA lyu-BIM-itsa
Мой любимчик/моя любимица

Sunshine
SOL-nish-ko
Солнышко

My love!
lyu-BOV mo-YA!
Любовь моя!

Hunny bunny
ZAI-ka
Зайка

My little cutie
mo-YA LA-poch-ka
Моя лапочка

Are you free tonight?
ti svo-BOD-na se-VOD-nya VE-che-rom?
Ты свободна сегодня вечером?
This is also in the feminine form. If you want to ask a guy, just subsitute свободен (*svo-BO-den*).

Hey, honey, wanna go…?
eh, kra-SOT-ka, nye KHO-chesh po-i-TI…?
Эй, красотка, не хочешь пойти…?
As above, use красавчик (*kra-SAV-chik*) if you're talking to a guy.

> **on a date**
> *na svi-DAN-i-ye*
> на свидание

back to my place
ko mnye do-MOI
ко мне домой

to the movies tonight
se-VOD-nya v ki-NO
сегодня в кино

to a dance club
na dis-KACH
на дискач

to a new club with me
so mnoi v NO-vii klub
со мной в новый клуб

My **girlfriend** is coming over tonight to hang out.
mo-YA GYORL-frend se-VOD-nya pri-DYOT po-obSCHAT-sya.
Моя **гёрлфренд** сегодня придёт пообщаться.
Sometimes you might hear this shortened to гёрла (*GYOR-la*).

My **boyfriend** brought me dinner.
moy boi-FREND pri-NES mne UZH-in.
Мой **бойфренд** принес мне ужин.

I just can't seem to forget my **old flame**.
ya ni-KAK nye mo-GU za-BIT svo-YU bIV-shu-yu PA-ssi-yu.
Я никак не могу забыть свою **бывшую пассию**.

You're the best **lover (male)** I've ever had.
ti SA-mii LU-chshii lyu-BOV-nik, ko-TO-rii u me-NYA kogDA-LI-bo bil.
Ты самый лучший **любовник**, который у меня когда-либо был.

The whole time they were married, he had a **lover (female)** on the side.
vsyo VRE-mya, kog-DA o-NI BI-li zhen-A-ti, u nye-VO bil-A lyu-BOV-nitsa na sto-ro-NYE.
Всё время, когда они были женаты, у него была **любовница** на стороне.

I met my **fiancée** through the Internet.

*ya po-zna-KO-mil-sya so svo-YEI **ne-VYE-stoi** CHE-rez in-ter-NET.*

Я познакомился со своей **невестой** через Интернет.

Russians use невеста for both "fiancée" and "bride" and жених for both "fiancé" and "groom."

My **fiancé** and I just registered at ZAGS.

*mi s mo-IM **zhe-ni-KHOM** TOL-ko chto za-re-gi-STRI-rova-lis v ZAG-sye.*

Мы с моим **женихом** только что зарегистрировались в ЗАГСе.

Couples in Russia are officially engaged once they've registered at this Soviet-style marriage hall. This is also where the civil ceremony takes place.

....

Queer culture
kvir-kul-TUR-a
Квир-Культура

Man, it sucks to be gay in Putin's Russia. Don't get me wrong, there was never really a good time to be gay in Russia, unless it was around the turn of the 20th century when all kinds of crazy shit went on, but probably no time since. Now, however, bad has gotten so much worse, as there are some astoundingly medieval laws railing against "gay propaganda and the corruption of youth." So if you're gay in Russia, you're better off keeping that shit to yourself unless you're with someone you know really well. And even then, reactions can be unpredictable. That's not to say that there aren't fairly out LGBT (ЛГБТ/*el-ge-be-te*) folks, but they risk their safety daily. Fortunately, the Internet is more progressive than daily life, and there are some online outlets for queer culture to thrive (or survive, at least). The biggest site is the aptly named gay.ru, but kvir.ru is pretty popular, too, and seems to be updated more frequently. Gay slang is called хабальство (*kha-BAL-stvo*), and if you "sound gay," that's called хабалить (*kha-BA-lit*), which, if you're a dude, means you use a lot of elongated vowels and female-gendered words to refer to yourself. If you do, however, nasty people may say you belong in Гейропа (*gay-RO-pa*), which is how they refer to the Sodom and Gomorrah they imagine Western Europe to be.

Homosexual
go-mo-syeks-u-a-LIST
Гомосексуалист
This is a neutral term.

Gay
go-lu-BOI
Голубой
A neutral term which, in most other contexts, means "light blue." It is also increasingly common to hear the English word "gay" (гей) being used.

Pederast
pye-de-RAST
Педераст
The retort to this is гетераст (*gye-te-RAST*), gay slang for a breeder (or straight person).

Homo
GO-mik
Гомик

Fag
PYE-dik
Педик
This is a pretty offensive term.

Faggot
PI-dor
Пидор
Also an offensive term.

Homophobe
go-mo-FOB
Гомофоб

Straights
na-tu-RA-ly
Натуралы

Top
ak-TIV
Актив

Bottom
pas-SIV
Пассив

Versatile
u-ni-ver-SAL
Универсал
Or уни (*U-ni*) for short.

Straight-acting
ne-MA-ner-nii
Неманерный

Gay marriage
gay-brak
Гей-брак
In media designed for straight people, the more-often-used term is
однополый брак (*od-no-POL-nii brak*), or same-sex marriage.

To come out
so-vyer-SHIT ka-min-OUT
Совершить камин-аут
The old term for this, which you may still hear, is уйти из подполья (*u-i-TI
iz pod-PO-lya*), or to come out from underground.

Transvestite
trans-vyes-TIT
Трансвестит

Transgender

trans-GEN-der

Трансгендер

Also, you will hear транссексуал (*tran-syeks-u-AL*) for FtM and транссексуалка (*tran-syeks-u-al-ka*) for MtF.

Do you know where I can find a **go-go bar**?

ty ne ZNA-yesh gdye bi na-i-TI **go-go bar**?

Ты не знаешь где бы найти **го-го бар**?

I'd really like to go to a **gay club**.

mnye bi O-chen kho-TYE-los po-i-TI v **gei KLUB**.

Мне бы очень хотелось пойти в **гей клуб**.

Moscow has a pretty active **gay scene**.

v mosk-VYE do-STA-toch-no ak-TIV-na-ya **go-lu- BYAT-nya**.

В Москве достаточно активная **голубятня**.

Where is the best **cruising street** in this city?

gdye SA-ma-ya LU-chsha-ya **PLYE-shka v** *E-tom GOro-dye?*

Где самая лучшая **плешка** в этом городе?

Also sometimes called панель (*pa-NYEL*).

Every big city has a **queer quarter**.

v KAZH-dom bol-SHOM GO-ro-dye yest **go-mo-DROM**.

В каждом большом городе есть **гомодром**.

Lesbian

lyes-bi-YAN-ka

Лесбиянка

Dyke

RO-zo-va-ya

Розовая

Literally, "pink."

Lesbo

LYES-bi

Лесби

Carpet muncher
LI-za
Лиза

A newbie vagitarian
nu-lye-VA-ya GYOR-la
Нулевая гёрла
Literally, a "zero girl."

Could you tell me the way to the nearest **taco stand?**
ti mnye nye pod-SKA-zhesh, kak do-BRAT-sya do bliZHAI-shevo
LYES-bi-scha?
Ты мне не подскажешь, как добраться до ближайшего
лесбища?

....

Characters
per-so-NA-zhi
Персонажи

It takes all kinds, and Russia is full of 'em! Here are some of
the many people you run the risk of meeting on the wild
streets of Moscow.

He thinks he's a **total badass** because he rides a hog.
*on schi-TA-yet se-BYA **kru-TIM PAR-nyem**, po-to-MU chto YEZ-dit na*
BAI-kye.
Он считает себя **крутым парнем**, потому что ездит на байке.

I know that **gigolo** is just using her for her money.
*ya ZNA-yu, chto E-tot **al-FONS** ye-YO i-SPOL-zu-yet PRO-sto RA-di*
DYEN-yeg.
Я знаю, что этот **альфонс** её использует просто ради денег.

That **jezebel** ruined his life.
*E-ta **di-na-MIST-i-ka** is-POR-ti-la ye-MU zhizn.*
Эта **динамистка** испортила ему жизнь.

That **computer geek** is always wrapped up in his programs.
tot kom-PYU-ter-schik po-sto-YA-nno za-vi-SA-yet za pro-GRA-mma-mi.
Тот **компьютерщик** постоянно зависает за программами.

Those **old geezers** spend their pension on vodka.
E-tot star-PYOR-ov TRA-tit svo-YU PYEN-si-yu na VODku.
Этот **старпёров** тратит свою пенсию на водку.

Those **old ladies** are always gossiping about me in the stairwell.
E-ti sta-RU-khi po-sto-YA-nno SPLYET-ni-cha-yut obo MNYE v pod-YEZ-dye.
Эти **старухи** постоянно сплетничают обо мне в подъезде.

That **gamer** never leaves his computer.
E-tot GEI-mer ot komp-A nye ot-KHO-dit.
Этот **геймер** от компа не отходит.

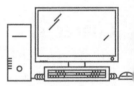

I'm looking for a **sugar daddy**.
ya i-SCHU se-BYE SPON-so-ra.
Я ищу себе **спонсора**.

Even though he's married, he's still an incurable **skirt chaser**.
nye-smo-TRYA na TO, chto zhe-NAT, on BAB-nik nye-izle-CHI-mii.
Несмотря на то, что женат, он **бабник** неизлечимый.

That **old maid** still lives with her mother.
E-ta STAR-a-ya DYE-va do sikh POR zhi-VYOT so svoYEI MA-ter-yu.
Эта **старая дева** до сих пор живёт со своей матерью.
In Russia, an old maid is any woman who's over 25 and still single.

I would never marry a **mama's boy**.
ya bi ni-kog-DA nye VI-shla ZA-muzh za MA-men-ki-no-vo SIN-ka.
Я бы никогда не вышла замуж за **маменькиного сынка**.

Thirtysomething woman
ZHEN-schi-na bal-ZA-kov-sko-vo VO-zrast-a
Женщина бальзаковского возраста
If you want to know more about what this is, there's a popular Russian TV show of the same name. It's a takeoff of *Sex and the City*, only Muscofied.

That **daddy's girl** always wears Gucci.
E-ta PA-pin-kin-a DOCH-ka vseg-DA NO-sit GU-chi.
Эта **папинкина дочка** всегда носит Гуччи.

My little brother is such a **snotty kid**.
moi MLAD-shii brat—MA-lyen-kii chpok.
Мой младший брат—**маленький чпок**.

I almost shat myself when I found out that she's **jailbait**.
ya chut ne ob-o-SRAL-sya kog-DA uz-NAL, chto on-A ma-lo-LYET-ka.
Я чуть не обосрался когда узнал, что она **малолетка**.

My **teenage** friends are always slacking off after school.
mo-I dru-ZYA-ti-NEi-je-ri vseg-DA byez-DYEL-ni-cha-yut PO-sle SHKOL-i.
Мои друзья-**тинэйджеры** всегда бездельничают после школы.

This **energizer bunny** goes jogging every morning.
E-tot e-ner-JAi-zer KAZH-do-ye U-tro na pro-BYEZHkye.
Этот **энерджайзер** каждое утро на пробежке.

That **hippie** walks around barefoot all day.
E-tot KHI-ppi KHO-dit TSE-lii dyen bo-si-KOM.
Этот **хиппи** ходит целый день босиком.

I can't believe how many **bums** there are in Moscow!
nye mo-GU VYER-it, STOL-ko yest bom-ZHEI v moskVYE!
Не могу поверить, столько есть **бомжей** в Москве!

Do you know where I can meet some local **punks?**
ti nye ZNA-yesh, gdye MO-zhno po-zna-KOM-it-sya s MYEST-ni-mi PANK-a-mi?
Ты не знаешь, где можно познакомиться с местными **панками**?

That **slacker** just goofs off all day.
E-tot byez-DYEL-nik TSE-lii dyen za-ni-MA-ye-tsya yerun-DOI.
Этот **бездельник** целый день занимается ерундой.

I think that **skinhead** is a follower of Barkashov.

po-MO-ye-mu E-tot skin DRU-zhit s bar-ka-SHOV-im.

По-моему этот **скин** сторонник Баркашова.

Alexander Barkashov is the former leader of the radical nationalist political group RNE (Russian National Unity), which attracted skinhead followers based on its agenda of ridding Russia of "foreigners and Jews."

That **hick** has never seen nothin' but dung.

E-tot kol-KHOZ-nik KRO-mye na-VO-za ni-che-VO v ZHIZ-ni nye VI-dyel.

Этот **колхозник** кроме навоза ничего в жизни не видел.

Literally, this means "collective farmer," but can describe any country-bumpkin type.

She's a total **fangirl**.

o-NA vo-ob-SHCE fan-GYORL-a.

Она вообще **фангёрла**.

That **hooligan** jacked my wallet!

E-tot khu-li-GAN SPIZ-dil moi ko-shel-OK!

Этот **хулиган** спиздил мой кошелёк!

This is the general Russian term describing anyone from a loudmouthed drunk to a gangbanger.

No one respects the **cops** in Russia.

ni-KTO nye u-va-ZHA-yet myent-OV v ro-SSII.

Никто не уважает **ментов** в России.

Those damned **bikers** are causing problems again.

E-ti pro-KLYA-ti-ye BAI-ke-ri
o-PYAT pro-BLYE-mi sozda-YUT.

Эти проклятые **байкеры** опять
проблемы создают.

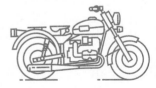

He's a **loser**.

on nye-u-DACH-nik.

Он **неудачник**.

Although the English word "loser" (лузер) has also arisen in recent years.

Only in Russia
TOL-ko v ro-SSII
только в России

New Russian
NO-vii RU-sskii
Новый русский
These are the guys who made a whole lotta dough on dubious business ventures and now drive around in expensive *inomarki*, own sweet dachas in *podmoskovie*, vacation in Ibiza, and yet still talk like the Russian version of Rocky Balboa. Their offspring are sometimes referred to as the Золотая молодёжь (*zo-lo-TA-ya mo-lo-DYOZH*), or "golden youth."

> That **New Russian** has a bitchin' black Beemer.
> *u E-to-vo NO-vo-vo RU-ssko-vo kru-TOI CHOR-nii BU-mer.*
> У этого **нового русского** крутой чёрный бумер.

Gangster
ban-DIT
Бандит
This word conjures up the seedy underworld of Russian crime. It can be used for low-level thieves and swindlers, but also for the Mafia boss–style gangsters. You will also hear the word гангстер (*GANG-ster*) used, too, for Mafia-types. On a related note, Russian has adopted the English word киллер (*KILL-er*), but this is used only for contract killers, not the more general murderers.

Russian intellectual
in-tye-lli-GYENT
Интеллигент
There's really no exact English equivalent for this word. It's similar to an intellectual, but one with particular interest in moral and social issues, often devoted to defending against the degradation of high culture and placing great importance on behaving properly. They are the polar opposite of the *noviye russkiye* and tend to feel a smug sense of moral superiority that is heightened by the abject poverty in which they often live. Nevertheless, интеллигентный (*in-tye-lli-GYENT-nii*) is just about the highest compliment you can give to a Russian over the age of 25.

That **intellectual** likes to sit in the kitchen all night and discuss philosophy.

E-tot in-tye-lli-GYENT LYU-bit si-DYET vsyu NOCH na KUKH-nye i ra-ssu-ZHDAT o fi-lo-SO-fii.

Этот **интеллигент** любит сидеть всю ночь на кухне и рассуждать о философии.

There's this whole thing in Russian culture, sometimes called "kitchen talk," where people (most often *intelligyenti*) sit in the kitchen all night and pontificate on the ills of society.

Mazhor

Ma-ZHOR

Мажор

The spoiled son of an influential and/or wealthy man. They pretty much get a free pass in life since *papochka* can always use his connections down at the ministry to get them out of any jam.

He's just a fucking **mazhor** whose daddy always pays his way.

on YO-ba-nnii ma-ZHOR, ko-TO-rii zhi-VYOT za PApin schot.

Он ёбаный **мажор**, который живёт за папин счёт.

Sovok

so-VOK

Совок

This term refers to someone with a Soviet mentality, and generally not in a complimentary way. These folks tend to spend most of their time complaining about capitalism and waxing nostalgic about Russia's former glory as a superpower. You can usually find them eating *shproty* under a portrait of Lenin in some rundown *kommunalka*, or complaining about the price of bread at any Soviet-style *produkty* store.

That **sovok** thinks that all foreigners are CIA secret agents.

E-tot so-VOK DU-ma-yet, chto VSYE i-no-STRANtsi—TAI-ni-ye a-GYEN-ti tse-er-U.

Этот **совок** думает, что все иностранцы—тайные агенты ЦРУ.

Pofigist

po-fig-IST

Пофигист

Someone who just doesn't give a shit about anything.

> That **pofigist** sleeps all day because he doesn't see the point of getting up.
>
> *E-tot po-fig-IST TSE-li-mi DNYA-mi spit, po-to-MU chto ne VI-dit SMI-sla vsta-VAT.*
>
> Этот **пофигист** целыми днями спит, потому что не видит смысла вставать.

Thug

GOP-nik

Гопник

A *gopnik* is the Russian version of a thug. He spends his time drinking vodka out of plastic cups and spitting sunflower seed shells all over the sidewalk on which he tends to squat. Once drunk, there is the potential for petty crimes or fighting. There seem to be fewer of them these days in Moscow, but believe me, there is no shortage out in the provinces.

> Only **thugs** party at that club.
>
> *v E-tom KLU-bye tu-SU-yu-tsya TOL-ko **GOP-ni-ki.***
>
> В этом клубе тусуются только **гопники**.

Ex-con

zek

Зек

This is the former inmate of a prison camp, and the term comes from the abbreviation for заключённый каналоармеец (*za-klu-CHYO-nnii ka-na-lo-ar-MYE-yets*). It's a pretty Soviet-era term, but these dudes are still around. Probably the easiest way to spot a zek is by his tattoos: Although tats have become popular in recent years among young people, they were traditionally a part of prison culture in Russia. Prison tats, however, usually involve coded symbols that, if correctly interpreted, can tell you which crimes the person has committed and what kind of time he served, among other interesting biographical facts.

> Judging by his tattoos, he's an **ex-con**.
>
> *SU-dya po ye-VO ta-tu-ir-OV-kam, on—zek.*
>
> Судя по его татуировкам, он—**зэк**.

Student life

stu-DYEN-ches-ka-ya zhizn

Студенческая жизнь

The Russian academic year is divided into two parts, called сессия (*sessiya*): зимняя сессия (*ZIM-nya-ya SYE-ssi-ya*) and весенняя сессия (*vye-SYE-nya-ya SYEssi-ya*). Each *sessiya* is followed by an exam period called экзаменационная сессия (*ek-za-men-a-tsi-ONN-ay-a SYE-ssi-ya*). Russian doesn't really have words for freshman, sophomore, etc.; instead, they just say на первом курсе (first year/*na PYER-vom KUR-sye*), на втором курсе (second year/*na vto-ROM KUR-sye*), and so on.

High school education through 9th grade

nye-POL-no-ye SRYED-ne-ye o-bra-zo-VA-ni-ye

Неполное среднее образование

After 9th grade, you have the option of leaving school and learning a trade. Or just smoking pot all day.

High school education through 11th grade

POL-no-ye SRYED-ne-ye o-bra-zo-VA-ni-ye

Полное среднее образование

Russian secondary schools go through 11 grades, so this is someone who has completed his secondary education and actually harbors some ambition in life.

Any educational institute beyond high school

VUZ

ВУЗ

This is the abbreviation for высшее учебное заведение (*VIsshe-ye u-CHEB-no-ye za-ve-DYE-ni-ye*), which means something like institute of higher learning and refers to anything post–high school.

Vo-tech
peh-teh-U
ПТУ

This stands for Профессионально-техническое училище (*pro-fye-ssi-o-NAL-no-tyekh-NI-che-sko-ye u-CHI-li-sche*) and is usually for the kids not really cut out for schoolin'.

> **Those vo-tech students just drink beer all day.**
> *E-ti pe-te-U-shni-ki TOL-ko PI-vo pyut TSEL-ii dyen.*
> Эти пэтэушники только пиво пьют целый день.

College
KO-llej
Колледж

A college is considered less prestigious than a университет (*u-nivyer-si-TYET*), or university.

Uni
u-ni-VYER
Универ

This abbreviated form is often used informally.

Grad school
a-spi-ran-TU-ra
Аспирантура

> **You'll never get into grad school with those grades!**
> *ti ni-kog-DA nye po-STU-pish v **a-spi-ran-TU-ru** s ta-KImi o-TSEN-ka-mi!*
> Ты никогда не поступишь в **аспирантуру** с такими оценками!

I got an A without taking the final.
*ya po-lu-CHIL pya-TYOR-ku **av-to-MAT-om**.*
Я получил пятёрку **автоматом**.

By the way, the Russian grading system is a five-point scale. 5 is called a пятёрка (*pya-TYOR-ka*) and is the equivalent of an A. It goes down from there. 4 is a четвёрка (*chetVYOR-ka*); 3 is a тройка (*TROI-ka*) and is the lowest grade you can get and still pass. 2 is a двойка (*DVOI-ka*) and is a failing grade. 1 is essentially never given unless a teacher has a real personal grudge against a student. Plus, it's possible to get a grade for a class without taking a final exam (*av-to-MAT*/Автомат).

Study nerd

bo-TAN
Ботан
Short for ботаник (*bo-TAN-ik*).

Total slacker student

stye-RIL-nii
Стерильный
This is the opposite of the ботан. He just always comes unprepared and has, on some level, accepted his fate as a failure.

The very first semester of one's college career

bo-ye-VO-ye kre-SCHE-ni-ye
Боевое крещение
The more standard meaning of this funny, slang term is "baptism by fire."

The halfway mark in your college degree program

ek-VA-tor
Экватор

Cheat sheet

SHPOR-a
Шпора
Short for шпаргалка (*shpar-GAL-ka*). There's also a type of cheat sheet called Бомба (*BOM-ba*) that has answers to the exact questions on the test.

Student ticket

stu-DAK
Студак
Short for студенческий билет (*stu-DYEN-ches-kii bi-LYET*). When Russian students take exams, they must randomly draw a "ticket." Whatever question is written on the ticket is what they must answer for their final exam grade. Unless their parents have a lot of money.

CHAPTER 3

Booze, Bars, & Clubs

VY-piv-ka, BA-ry, i KLU-by

Выпивка, Бары, и Клубы

The legends of Russian drinking are not exaggerated. They are hard-core drinkers. Bacchanalian revelry pervades all aspects of life, whether it's as a quick beer on the way to work, liquid lunches and vodka-drenched business meetings, or all-night parties that rapidly degenerate into reckless binging that blurs all lines between Friday night and Monday morning with a foggy haze of excess and regret. Let's face it: If you hang with Russians, you will drink. A lot. And in all likelihood, it will be at the most inappropriate times and in the most inappropriate places.

Tying one on

o-pya-NYE-ni-ye

Опьянение

I need a drink.

kho-CHU VI-pit.

Хочу выпить.

Let's go ...
poi-DYOM ...
Пойдём ...

> **boozing**
> *DYOR-nem*
> дёрнем

> **get wasted**
> *po-bu-KHAT*
> побухать

> **party**
> *za-zhi-GAT*
> зажигать

> **do some drinkin'**
> *BAKH-nut*
> бахнуть

> **get smashed**
> *na-ZHRYOM-sya*
> нажрёмся

I want to get drunk.
kho-CHU na-PIT-sya.
Хочу **напиться**.

I'm jonesing for a drink.
TRU-bi gor-YAT.
Трубы горят.

Pour 'em!
na-li-VAI!
Наливай!

Let me get this round.
da-VAI ya za-bosh-LYA-yu.
Давай я забошляю.

I demand that the banquet continue!
ya TRYE-bu-yu pro-dol-ZHE-ni-ya ban-KYE-ta!
Я требую продолжения банкета!
Score some cultural points with this famous line from the classic Soviet comedy Иван Васильевич меняет профессию (*Ivan Vasilievich Changes Professions*).

Where Russians get drunk
gdye RU-sski-ye na-pi-VA-yu-tsya
Где русские напиваются

Russians drink everywhere. Bars and clubs are all around, from dives hidden away in piss-soaked basements to upscale establishments full of flat-headed thugs in leather jackets and bouncers checking weapons at the door. When in Russia, choose your watering hole wisely!

Let's go ...
poi-DYOM ...
Пойдём ...
Remember when talking about direction, you need to use the accusative case.

to a bar
v bar
в бар

to a strip joint
na strip-TIZ
на стриптиз

to a booze bash
na bu-KHA-lo-vo
на бухалово

to a club
v klub
в клуб

to a dance club
na dis-ko-TYE-ku
на дискотеку

to my place
ko MNYE
ко мне

Let's drink …
da-VAi VI-pyem …
Давай выпьем …

on the street
na U-li-tse
на улице

in a park
v PAR-kye
в парке

in a stairwell
v pod-YEZ-dye
в подъезде

with some hos I know
u zna-KOM-ikh BLYA-dyei
у знакомых блядей

There's going to be a rockin' **party** tonight.
se-VOD-nya BU-dyet KLASS-na-ya tu-SOV-ka.
Сегодня будет классная **тусовка**.

Are you going to the **afterparty**?
ti poi-DYOSH na after-PAR-ti?
Ты пойдёшь на **афтерпати**?
Sometimes just called an АП (ah-PE).

Me and my buds are going for a **guys' night out**.
mi so svo-I-mi re-BYA-ta-mi i-DYOM na mal-CHISH-nik.
Мы со своими ребятами идём на **мальчишник**.

My girlfriend went to a **girls' night out** tonight while I sat at home like an idiot.
po-KA ya TU-po si-DYEL DO-ma, mo-YA DYEV-ush-ka po-SHLA na dyev-ICH-nik.
Пока я тупо сидел дома, моя девушка пошла на **девичник**.

The night is young.
VRE-mya DYET-sko-ye.
Время детское.

....

Booze
bu-KHLO
Бухло

Not surprisingly, the Russian drink of choice is vodka, most often shot straight up. Beer is becoming increasingly popular with the younger crowd, however, and many bars now offer both local and imported brews on tap.

Since Russia is in love with the stupid metric system, you order vodka in measurements of 50 grams, which is just about 2 ounces (a typical American shot is an ounce and a half). So you can order as little as one small 50-gram drink (пятьдесят грамм/*pya-de-SYAT gramm*) or—more likely—a 500-gram bottle (пол-литра/*pol-LIT-ra*). The standard shot, however, is 100 grams (сто грамм/*sto gramm*), sometimes just called a стопка (*STOP-ka*). For beer, you order by the parts of a liter—most commonly a third (called ноль три/ *nol tri*) or a half (called ноль пять/ *nol pyat*), and you can actually buy up to 2.5 liters of beer in big plastic bottles as if it were soda. This is called a базука (*ba-ZU-ka*).

What are we having?
chto BU-dyem?
Что будем?

I'll have....
ya BU-du....
Я буду....
Notice that all of these words are in the accusative case.

> **vodka**
> *VOD-ku*
> водку

> **voddy**
> *VO-doch-ku*
> водочку
> An affectionate term for vodka. You may also hear the term водяра (*vo-DYAR-a*).

> **moonshine**
> *sa-mo-GON*
> самогон
> Although the real sots just call this Russian home brew сэм (*sem*).

> **pure grain alcohol**
> *chi-sto-GAN*
> чистоган

> **beer**
> *piv-KO*
> пивко

> **yorsh**
> *yorsh*
> ёрш
> A mixed drink consisting of vodka and beer.

beer and sour cream
PI-vo so smye-TA-noi
пиво со сметаной
Before there was Viagra, there was beer and sour cream.

wine
vin-TSO
винцо

mulled wine
glint-VYEIN
глинтвейн

home-brewed fruit wine
GRU-shki-YA-bloch-ki
грушки-яблочки

CHASERS
ZA-KU-SO-NI
ЗАКУСОНЫ

The Russian idea of a chaser is a lot more liberal than the American version. Although chasing vodka with fruit juice is possible, pounding down *sto gramm* will be followed more often by a swig of beer, by a bite of a pickle, or by sniffing a piece of black bread. It'll burn at first, but much to your own undoing, it'll get easier with each passing shot.

What can I **chase** with?
chem za-ku-SIT?
Чем закусить?

What can I **take a whiff** of (to kill the burn)?
chem za-NYU-khat?
Чем занюхать?

Let's **chase with some beer.**
da-VAI piv-KOM shli-fo-NYOM-sya.
Давай пивком шлифонёмся.

port

port-VEIN

портвейн

It's cheap, it's potent, and it's also sometimes called портвешок (*port-ve-SHOK*).

bubbly

sham-PUN

шамнунь

This literally means "shampoo," so it's all about the context here.

a cocktail

kok-TYEIL

коктейль

a screwdriver

ot-VYOR-ku

отвёртку

a bloody Mary

kro-VA-vu-yu ME-ri

кровавую Мэри

a gin and tonic

dzhin TO-nik

джин тоник

a rum and Coke

rom KO-lu

ром колу

cognac

ko-NYAK

коньяк

The more slangy word is конина (*ko-NI-na*). This is, of course, more often brandy than actual cognac.

Do you have (dark, light) beer **on tap**?
*YEST u vas (TYOM-no-ye, SVYET-lo-ye) PI-vo **na roz-LIvye**?*
Есть у вас (тёмное, светлое) пиво **на розливе**?

It's time to move on to **something stronger**.
*po-RA **pod-NYAT GRA-dus**.*
Пора **поднять градус**.

That bartender **mixes** a mean drink.
*E-tot bar-MEN **ba-DYA-zhit** KLASS-ni-ye kok-TYEI-li.*
Этот бармен **бадяжит** классные коктейли.

We'll drink anything that burns.
mi pyom VSYO, chto go-RIT.
Мы пьём всё, что горит.

I'm not going to drink this **shitty** beer.
*ya nye BU-du pit E-to **pi-zdo-VA-to-ye** PI-vo.*
Я не буду пить это **пиздоватое** пиво.

This is **crappy** vodka.
*E-ta VOD-ka **khre-NO-va-ya**.*
Эта водка **хреновая**.

This **home brew** really packs a punch.
*E-tot **sem** da-YOT ZHA-ru.*
Этот **сэм** даёт жару.

Let's have **another round**.
*da-VAI **e-SCHO po od-NOI**.*
Давай **ещё по одной**.

What, have you lost your fucking mind? We've already drunk
half a barrel!
*ti CHTO, o-khu-YEL? mi u-ZHE **pol-BOCH-ki** VI-pi-li!*
Ты что, охуел? Мы уже **полбочки** выпили!

Gimme some **coins** for beer.
*go-NI mnye **BAB-ki** na PI-vo.*
Гони мне **бабки** на пиво.

Give me some dough.
dai ba-BLO.
Дай бабло.

Toasts
TOS-ti
Тосты

The more drunk Russians get, the longer and more tear-filled their toasts seem to be. But don't sweat it: It's not so much what you say, but the heart you put into it that will win over your drinking buddies. Most Russian toasts begin with variations of the following words:

Let's drink to...
da-VAI VI-pyem za...
Давай выпьем за...

Here's to...
da-VAI za...
Давай за...

> **meeting under the table!**
> *VSTRYE-chu pod sto-LOM!*
> встречу под столом!
> If you drink enough, this is where you ultimately wind up.

> **women. We don't care what we drink to anyway, and it makes them happy.**
> *ZHEN-schin. NAM-to vsyo rav-NO, za CHTO pit, a IM-pri-YAT-no.*
> женщин. Нам-то всё равно, за что пить, а им приятно.

> **a light heart and heavy pockets!**
> *LYO-gko-ye SYERD-tse i tya-ZHO-li-ye kar-MA-ni!*
> лёгкое сердце и тяжёлые карманы!

honest and humble people. There are so few of us left!
CHYES-nikh i SKROM-nikh lyu-DYEI. nas o-STA-los tak MA-lo!
честных и скромных людей. Нас осталось так мало!

wives and lovers, and to them never meeting.
zhon i lyu-BOV-nits, CHTO-bi on-i ni-kog-DA nye VSTRYE-ti-lis.
жён и любовниц, чтобы они никогда не встретились.

Wasted
bu-KHOI
Бухой

There will inevitably come a point when you're too drunk to slur out the words to demand another round. Not to worry: Just do as the Russians do and flick your middle finger against the side of your neck. You'll have your *sto gramm* in no time!

I'm fucked up beyond all recognition.
mnye POL-nii piz-DYETS.
Мне полный пиздец.
This doesn't just refer to being drunk, but can mean "I'm totally fucked" in just about any sense.

He's/She's ...
on/o-NA ...
Он/она ...

>   **drunk**
>   *PYA-nii/PYA-na-ya*
>   пьяный/пьяная

>   **a little tipsy**
>   *slye-GKA pyan/pya-NA*
>   слегка пьян/пьяна

SOME FINER POINTS OF RUSSIAN IMBIBING
NYU-AN-SI RUSS-KO-VO PYAN-STVA
НЮАНСЫ РУССКОГО ПЬЯНСТВА

Russians waste no time pounding down the drinks. By tradition, the first shot is quickly followed by the second. A popular Russian saying goes: Между первой и второй перерывчик небольшой (*MYEZH-du PYER-voi i vto-ROI pye-rye-RIV-chik nye-bol-SHOI*) or "You don't take a break between the first and the second shots." Keep in mind that Russian parties are a bit different from Americans parties. There is no mingling. When you go to a Russian party, you sit, you eat, and you drink. И всё (*I vsyo*). Here are other useful phrases:

Down the hatch!
do DNA!
До дна!
This is generally how you'll be cheered on when pounding down shots.

Brudershaft
Брудершафт
This is a toast honoring the brotherhood of men, in which you will be expected to link arms with the guy next to you as you gaze deeply into each other's increasingly dilated pupils and pound down another shot. Bottoms up!

A penalty drink
shtraf-NOI
Штрафной
These are awarded so that any latecomers don't stay sober long enough to gather compromising information on their already-shitfaced and loose-lipped companions.

One for the road
na po-so-SHOK
На посошок
This is traditionally the last toast of the evening. Drink it down and get out while you still can!

And on a final note, there is a Russian custom of immediately removing empty bottles from the table. This often means placing them on the floor, under or beside the table. I'm not entirely sure why they do this: It may be superstition related, or it might just be a not-so-subtle hint that they are ready for another bottle to be opened.

shitfaced drunk
v SRA-ku pyan/pya-NA
в сраку пьян/пьяна

drunk off his/her ass
v ZHO-pu pyan/pyan-A
в жопу пьян/пьяна

wrecked
pyan/pya-NA v khlam
пьян/пьяна в хлам

wasted
bu-KHOI/bu-KHA-ya
бухой/бухая

already three sheets to the wind
u-zZHE le-TA-yet
уже летает

feeling no pain
kho-ROSH/kho-ro-SHA
хорош/хороша

on a bender
v za-PO-ye
в запое

....

Drinkers
PYU-schi-ye
Пьющие

It ain't hard to find someone to drink with in Russia.

Drinking buddy
so-bu-TIL-nik
Собутыльник

A drunkard
PYA-ni-tsa
Пьяница

An alcoholic
al-ko-GO-lik
Алкоголик

A wino
BU-khar
Бухарь

An alkie
al-KASH
Алкаш

That **fucking alkie** always wants to mooch drinks.
E-tot YO-ba-nnii al-KASH vsyeg-DA KHO-chet na SHAru pit.
Этот **ёбанный алкаш** всегда хочет на шару пить.

The cops
men-TI
менты

Although public drunkenness is common in Russia, attracting too much attention to yourself could run you the risk of an unpleasant encounter with some of Russia's finest, out trolling for a little supplementary income. Have your passport on hand, carry some spare cash, and practice saying these words so that you can express your righteous indignation the next day among your comrades.

Cops
men-TI
Менты

Po-po
lye-GA-vii
Легавый

The fuzz
myen-TYA-ra
Ментяра

The pigs picked me up. Those bitches!
mu-so-RA me-NYA za-gre-BLI. SU-ki!
Мусора меня загребли. Суки!
This is what the real badasses call the po-po.

That new guy totally narced me out to **the 5-0.**
E-tot gni-LOI me-NYA za-svye-TIL dush-MA-nu.
Этот гнилой меня засветил **душману.**
This term is mainly used by druggies.

The cops made me pay **a fine** for being a public nuisance.
men-TI za-STA-vi-li za-pla-TIT shtraf za khu-li-GAN-stvo.
Менты заставили заплатить **штраф** за хулиганство.
Though of course, "fine" is just a euphemism for what it really is: a bribe
(Взятка/ *VZYAT-ka*).

If you get caught with that shit, they'll **send you up the river.**
YES-li ob-na-RU-zhit te-BYA s E-toi DRYA-nyu, to te-BYA po-SA-dyat na kich-MAN.
Если обнаружат тебя с этой дрянью, то **тебя посадят на кичман.**

Russia is just **completely whack.**
v ro-SSII POL-nii byes-prye-DYEL.
В России полный **беспредел.**
Byespryedyel is a slang word right out of the big house, now used to
describe the chaotic lawlessness and corruption pervading Russian
society.

He did five years for **possession.**
on si-DYEL pyat lyet za khra-NYE-ni-ye.
Он сидел пять лет за **хранение.**

The hangover
pokh-MYE-lye
Похмелье

If you're hanging with Russians, this is gonna be a familiar state to you. My advice? Do as the Russians do: Suck it up and drink it off, and then promise yourself that you will never drink that much again. At least not until the weekend.

I'm **hungover.**
ya z bo-du-NA.
Я с **бодуна.**

I feel like shit.
me-NYA kol-BA-sit.
Меня колбасит.

My liver hurts.
PYE-chen bo-LIT.
Печень болит.

The room is **spinning.**
u me-NYA ver-to-LYO-ti.
У меня **вертолёты.**
Literally, "I have helicopters."

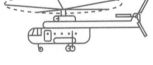

I have **dry mouth.**
u me-NYA sush-NYAK.
У меня **сушняк.**

I don't remember **a damn thing.**
ya ni fi-GA nye POM-nyu.
Я **ни фига** не помню.

Foul breath after a night of hard drinking
pe-re-GAR
Перегар

I feel nauseated by his stinky **day-after breath.**
men-YA tosh-NIT ot je-VO pe-re-GAR-a.
Меня тошнит от его **перегара**.

I need to **drink off this hangover** ASAP.
mnye NA-do SRO-chno o-pokh-mye-LIT-sya.
Мне надо срочно **опохмелиться**.

The hair of the dog
klin KLIN-om
Клин клином
You might also hear the phrase клин клином вышибают (*klin KLIN-om vy-shy-BA-yut*), which basically means, "You have to fight fire with fire."

It's OK, I'll **sleep it off.**
ni-che-VO, ya o-to-SPLYUS.
Ничего, я **отосплюсь**.
If you can't handle a morning eye-opener, another tried-and-true Russian method of curing a hangover is drinking pickle brine, or рассол (*ra-SSOL*).

....

Drugs
nar-KO-ti-ki
Наркотики

While drinking alcohol is still the great Russian national pastime, drugs can be scored in just about any Russian city, large or small. They have become a big part of the Moscow club scene, and ecstasy-fueled raves are some of the hottest tickets in town. But get caught with dope in Russia and you will be royally screwed. So if you don't have the balls for spending a few years sharing a shower with TB-ravaged serial killers and rapists, you might want to stick to the bottle. But, hey, no one's judging here. And so...

Dope

nar-ko-TA

Наркота

This can refer to any type of drugs, so be careful who you ask for *narkota*.

I've got **the goods** today.

u me-NYA se-VOD-nya pro-DUKT.

У меня сегодня **продукт**.

Let's get high.

da-VAI po-kai-FU-yem.

Давай покайфуем.

I'm jonesing hard.

ya go-LOD-nii.

Я голодный.

How much for **a bag**?

po-CHOM ba-LLON?

Почём **баллон**?

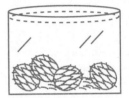

I don't know why he's looking **to score** when he's already **holding**.

mnye nye po-NYAT-no, za-CHEM on v raz-VYED-kye kog-DA on u-ZHE za-TA-re-nnii.

Мне не понятно, зачем он **в разведке**, когда он уже **затаренный**.

I'm sick of vodka—let's **get high** for a change.

mnye na-do-YE-la VOD-ka—da-VAI LU-chshe bakhNYOM-sya.

Мне надоела водка—давай лучше **бахнёмся**.

Every time he's high he gets the giggles.

KAZH-dii raz, kog-DA on v TOR-bye, on na khi-KHI podSA-zhi-va-yet-sya.

Каждый раз, когда он в торбе, он на хи-хи подсаживается.

I'm, like, totally stoned.

ya, TI-pa, po KAI-fu.

Я, типа, по кайфу.

He gets baked every chance he gets.
on LO-vit kaif pri lyu-BOI voz-MOZH-nosti.
Он ловит кайф при любой возможности.

Man, I hate coming down.
blin, ya nye-na-VI-zhu ot-kho-DYAK.
Блин, я ненавижу **отходняк**.

....

Where to score
gdye do-STAT
Где достать

Dealer
DI-ler
Дилер
In Russia, often someone from central Asia or the Caucasus, also
sometimes called a Бабай (*ba-BAI*), or Басурман (*ba-sur-MAN*).

Connection
go-NYETS
Гонец

**I need to find me a new hookup, mine doesn't know jack about
dope.**
mnye NA-do na-i-TI NO-vo-vo DOK-to-ra, moi—dva po KU-shu.
Мне надо найти нового **доктора**, мой—два по кушу.

Do you know where I can score around here?
ti nye ZNA-yesh gdye tut MOZH-no VI-ru-bat?
Ты не знаешь где тут можно **вырубать**?

Their hot spot is in an old communal apartment.
ikh kon-TOR-a na-KHO-dit-sya v STA-roi ko-mmu-NALkye.
Их **контора** находится в старой коммуналке.

Weed

trav-A

Трава

The funny thing about weed in Russia is where you'll find it growing. I once went to the Ryazan region dacha of a 60-year-old woman and saw a 5-foot-tall plant, and there used to be a few smaller hemp shrubs not far from one of the embassy buildings in Ukraine. Most people don't even know what it is, and those who do know don't bother because the quality is such crap. If you want the good stuff, go for something from Central Asia or the Caucasus.

Let's smoke some ...
da-VAI po-KU-rim ...
Давай покурим ...
Notice these words are all in the accusative.

marijuana
ma-ri-khu-A-nu
марихуану

pot
a-na-shU
анашу

grass
ZYE-lyen
зелень

bud
pye-TRUSH-ku
петрушку

cannabis
gan-dzhu-BAS
ганджубас

Russian golden leaf
A-tom
атом
Usually imported weed from places south such as Central Asia.

Hemp
ko-no-PLYA
Конопля

This **ganj** ain't good, but at least it's cheap.
E-tot ko-chi-BEI khrye-NO-vii, no khot dye-SHO-vii.
Этот **кочубей** хреновый, но хоть дешёвый.

These Russian **potheads** only smoke dirt grass.
E-ti RU-sski-ye PLA-ne-ri KUR-yat TOL-ko KLYE-ver.
Эти русские **планеры** курят только клевер.

Aren't there any **stoners** in Moscow?
nye-u-ZHE-li NYET-u u-PIKH-ti-shei v mosk-VYE?
Неужели нету **упыхтышей** в Москве?

Wanna buy a **dime bag**?
KHO-chesh ku-PIT GA-lich-ku?
Хочешь купить **галичку**?

Where can I get some **rolling papers**?
gdye MOZH-no do-STAT PO-pik?
Где можно достать **попик**?

Anybody got a **joint**?
u ko-VO-ni-BUD YEST ko-SYAK?
У кого-нибудь есть **косяк**?

Hey, man, let's **toke** this **roach**.
ei, pa-TSAN, da-VAI po-ku-MA-rim E-tot pye-GAS.
Эй, пацан, давай **покумарим** этот **пегас**.

Where did you put my **stash**?
gdye ti po-lo-ZHIL moi pa-KYET?
Где ты положил мой **пакет**?

Let's go buy some **logs**.
poi-DYOM KU-pim BYE-li-ki.
Пойдём купим **Белики**.
These are *papirosy* that can be hollowed out and filled with pot. The full name is Беломорканал (*bye-lo-mor-ka-NAL*).

Let's kill this one.
da-VAI PYAT-ku smi-NAT.
Давай пятку сминать.

Careful with my **bong**, dude.
chu-VAK, a-kku-RAT-no s mo-IM bul-bu-LYA-tor-om.
Чувак, аккуратно с моим **бульбулятором**.
Also sometimes just called а бонг (*bong*).

I smoked a joint and now I've got crazy **munchies**.
ya do-ku-rIl dol-BAN i tye-PYER MU-cha-yus ZHO-rom.
Я докурил Долбан и теперь **мучаюсь жором**.

Other drugs
dru-GI-ye nar-KO-ti-ki
Другие наркотики

Druggie
nar-ko-MAN
Наркоман

Heroin
gye-ro-IN
Героин

Smack
BYE-lii
Белый

Trippy drugs
vol-SHEB-ni-ki
Волшебники

LSD
el-es-DE
ЛСД

Acid
ki-slo-TA
Кислота

PCP
Well, it's just called PCP, although sometimes you'll hear the term
ангельская пыль (*AN-gyel-ska-ya pil*), or angel dust, just like back home.

Ecstasy
Ek-sta-zi
Экстази

Cocaine
ko-ka-IN
Кокаин

Blow
nyu-KHA-ra
Нюхара

Burnout
tor-CHOK
Торчок

Overdose
pye-rye-do-zi-ROV-ka
Передозировка

Let's drop some **Lucy** and go clubbing.
*da-VAI pro-glo-TIM **LYU-syu** i po-klu-BIM-sya.*
Давай проглотим **Люсю** и поклубимся.

Have you ever been to **a rave**?
*ti kog-DA-ni-BUD **bil na REI-vye**?*
Ты когда-нибудь был **на рейве**?

Do you know where I can score some **snow** around here?
ti nye ZNA-yesh, gdye MOZH-no VI-ru-bat tut snye-ZHOK?
Ты не знаешь, где можно вырубать тут **снежок**?

I'm not really into **kiddie doping**.
mnye nye O-chen NRA-vit-sya po ko-LYO-sam torCHAT.
Мне не очень нравится **по колесам торчать**.

I don't **shoot up H**.
ya nye VZHA-ri-va-yus GYE-ru.
Я не **вжариваюсь геру**.

She's a junkie.
o-NA si-DIT na i-GLYE.
Она сидит на игле.

He spends all his time **popping pills**.
on vsyo VRYE-mya za-KI-di-va-yet.
Он всё время **закидывает**.

I think I can get that **white coat** to write me a **script**.
po-MO-ye-mu ya smo-GU u-go-vo-RIT E-to lye-PI-lo mnye na-pi-SAT chye-KUSH-ku.
По-моему я смогу уговорить это **лепило** мне написать **чекушку**.

He just **got on** and already he's **getting hooked**.
on nye-DAV-no NA-chal na ZHA-lo ki-DAT i u-ZHE saDIT-sya.
Он недавно начал **на жало кидать** и уже **садится**.

He's permafried.
on v sis-TYE-mye.
Он в системе.

I don't think I can just **quit cold turkey**.
ya VRYAD li smo-gU na su-KHU-yu slyezt.
Я вряд ли смогу **на сухую слезть**.

I'm on the straight.
ya na ku-MA-rakh.
Я на кумарах.

CHAPTER 4

Sexy Body, Ugly Body

sek-su-AL-no-ye TYE-lo, u-ROD-li-vo-ye TYE-lo

Сексуальное тело, Уродливое тело

Though fast food is increasingly popular in the former Soviet Union, Russian bodies don't seem to have supersized the way that Americans have. Most young Russians are in great shape and don't start to fatten up until they're 50 or so. I think the secret is that they walk...a lot...and usually while carrying ridiculously heavy bags. Most Russians, particularly women, take a lot of pride in their appearance. Even a quick trip to the *rynok* requires a dress, heels, and full makeup. They like to look good for any occasion, and a big part of that is keeping their bodies in shape. Ain't nothing wrong with that!

Body

TYE-lo

Тело

He's got a nice **six pack**.
u nye-VO kho-RO-shii **pryess**.
У него хороший **пресс**.

He's got a big belly.
u nye-VO bol-SHO-ye PU-zo.
У него большое **пузо**.

She has amazing legs.
u nye-YO o-bal-DYE-nni-ye NO-zhki.
У неё **обалденные ножки**.

He's got a cute butt.
u nye-VO sim-pa-TICH-na-ya PO-pa.
У него **симпатичная попа**.

She's got a great chest.
u nye-YO KLASS-na-ya grud.
У неё **классная грудь**.

You've got beautiful eyes.
u te-BYA kra-SI-vi-ye gla-ZI-sche.
У тебя **красивые глазищи**.

She's got a pretty nice kisser.
u nye-YO nye-plo-KHA-ya mor-DASH-ka.
У неё неплохая **мордашка**.

He has a stupid mug.
u nye-VO tu-PA-ya MOR-da.
У него тупая **морда**.

I gave him one in the muzzle.
ya e-MU dal v ye-BAL-o.
Я ему дал в **ебало**.
This is a pretty offensive term for face as is ебальник (*ye-BAL-nik*).

He's bearded like a lumberjack.
on bo-ro-DA-tii kak dro-vo-SYEK.
Он **бородатый** как дровосек.

He's got a double chin.
u nye-VO vto-ROI pod-bo-RO-dok.
У него **второй подбородок**.

She's got **nasty saddlebags.**
u nye-YO pro-TIV-ni-ye U-shi na BYO-drakh.
У неё противные **уши на бёдрах.**

She has **big teeth** like a beaver.
o-NA zu-BA-sta-ya kak bo-BYOR.
Она **зубастая** как бобёр.

He has a **big schnozz.**
u nye-VO nos kar-TO-shkoi.
У него **нос картошкой.**

Her **ass** is so wide, it needs its own zip code.
ye-YO ZHO-pa na-STOL-ko shi-ro-KA, chto TRYE-bu-yet svo-ye-VO IN-dyek-sa.
Её **жопа** настолько широка, что требует своего индекса.

Sexy
SYE-ksi
Секси

I don't know what it is about the Slavs, but overall, they are a damn fine-looking people. High cheekbones, slightly Asian eyes, and those exotic rolled *r*'s—all together, they make for one sexy package.

Damn, you...!
blin, nu ti i...!
Блин, ну ты и...!

> **fine**
> *shi-KAR-nii/shi-KAR-na-ya*
> шикарный/шикарная
>
> **smokin'**
> *po-TRYAS-nii/po-TRYAS-na-ya*
> потрясный/потрясная

real cute
kho-RO-shen-kii/kho-RO-shen-ka-ya
хорошенький/хорошенькая

gorgeous
o-fi-GYE-nnii/o-fi-GYE-nna-ya
офигенный/офигенная

sexy
syeks-a-PIL-nii/syeks-a-PIL-na-ya
сексапильный/сексапильная

He's in really good shape.
on v O-chen kho-RO-shei FOR-mye.
Он в очень хорошей форме.

She's really built.
o-NA O-chen STROI-na-ya.
Она очень стройная.

He's such a stud.
on zhe-rye-BYETS.
Он жеребец.

You've got a fuckin' hot bod!
u te-BYA o-khu-YE-nna-ya fi-GU-ra!
У тебя охуенная фигура!

He's/she's a hottie.
on/o-NA kra-SAV-chik/kra-SOT-ka.
Он/Она красавчик/красотка.

She's real pretty.
o-NA smaz-LI-vyen-ka-ya.
Она смазливенькая.

He ain't bad!
da on ni-che-VO!
Да он ничего!

She is fucking hot!
o-NA ye-BLI-va-ya!
Она ебливая!

....

Ugly
u-ROD-li-vii
Уродливый

Because we can't all be born beautiful.

Damn, you...!
blin, nu ti i...!
Блин, ну ты и...!

> **hideous**
> *bye-zo-BRAZ-nii/bye-zo-BRAZ-na-ya*
> безобразный/безобразная
>
> **nasty**
> *PA-kost-nii/PA-kost-na-ya*
> пакостный/пакостная
>
> **gross**
> *pro-TIV-nii/pro-TIV-na-ya*
> противный/противная
>
> **disgusting**
> *ot-vra-TI-tyel-nii/ot-vra-TI-tyel-na-ya*
> отвратительный/отвратительная
>
> **fugly**
> *u-YO-bisch-nii/u-YO-bisch-na-ya*
> уёбищный/уёбищная

He needs to go on a diet.
ye-MU po-RA syest na di-YE-tu.
Ему пора сесть на диету.

She's a fucking skeleton.
o-NA khu-do-YO-bi-na.
Она худоёбина.

He's as hunchbacked as a camel.
on gor-BA-tii kak vyer-BLYUD.
Он горбатый как верблюд.

She's a four-eyes.
o-NA och-KAS-ta-ya.
Она очкастая.

He's as bug-eyed as a dragonfly.
u nye-VO gla-ZA na-VI-kat, kak u strye-koz-l.
У него глаза навыкат, как у стрекозы.

She's a bleached blonde.
o-NA KRA-she-nna-ya blon-DIN-ka.
Она крашенная блондинка.

She is butt ugly.
o-NA KLU-sha.
Она клуша.

She's a hairy mess.
o-NA do bye-zo-BRA-zi-ya vo-lo-SA-ta-ya.
Она до безобразия волосатая.

He's a fat ass.
on zho-PA-stii.
Он жопастый.

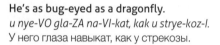

Illness
bo-LYEZN
Болезнь

Another, more cynical, explanation for those slender Russian bods is that many Russians are prone to illness.

Whether it's from the harsh climate, exposure to radiation and pollution, unbalanced nutrition, limited access to competent health care, or all the drinking and smoking most people seem to do, Russians seem to get sick a lot.

What's wrong with you?
CHTO s to-BOI?
Что с тобой?

I feel **really shitty.**
ya khrye-NO-vo se-BYA CHUST-vu-yu.
Я **хреново** себя чувствую.

I'd be better off dead.
zhi-VI-ye za-VI-du-yut MYORT-vim.
Живые завидуют мёртвым.
Literally, "the living envy the dead."

You look like crap.
ti khye-RO-vo VI-glya-dish.
Ты херово выглядишь.

My head is pounding.
bash-KA bo-LIT.
Башка болит.

I have **high blood pressure.**
u me-NYA vi-SO-ko-ye da-VLYE-ni-ye.
У меня высокое **давление**.
This is a fairly common complaint among old and young alike.

I've been **down in the dumps** all week.
u me-NYA TSE-lu-yu nye-DYE-liu dye-pryess-NYAK.
У меня целую неделю **депрессняк**.

I have **angina.**
u me-NYA an-GI-na.
У меня **ангина**.
This is something that Russians seem to complain about a lot. It usually just seems to be something along the lines of a sore throat.

IF YOU SIT ON CONCRETE, YOUR OVARIES WILL FREEZE
YES-LI PO-SI-DISH NA BE-TO-NYE, TO YA-ICH-NI-KI OT-MYOR-ZNUT
ЕСЛИ ПОСИДИШЬ НА БЕТОНЕ, ТО ЯИЧНИКИ ОТМЁРЗНУТ

If you ask Russians why they're sick, nine times out of ten they'll blame the weather, a problem involving atmospheric pressure, or the fact that they sat on concrete under a clear sky while not wearing a hat. Russians have some medical beliefs that will seem straight up bizarre to Westerners, but don't even try to argue with them about health. No matter how outlandish their claims, they will be convinced that they are right, and it will be a waste of time trying to change their minds. Here are some of the weird reasons why Russians think they get sick, and the even weirder cures they use to heal themselves.

A lot of people feel ill today because of the **atmospheric pressure**.
*MHO-gi-ye sye-VOD-nya bo-LE-yut iz-za **da-VLYE-ni-ya v at-moSFYER-ye**.*
Многие сегодня болеют из-за **давления в атмосфере**.

If you **sit in the draft**, you'll catch a cold.
*YES-li **po-si-DISH v skvoz-nya-KYE**, to pro-STU-dish-sya.*
Если **посидишь в сквозняке**, то простудишься.

I **had a drink with ice**, and now my throat hurts.
*ya **VI-pil na-PI-tok so l-DOM** i tye-PYER u me-NYA GOR-lo bo-LIT.*
Я **выпил напиток со льдом** и теперь у меня горло болит.

He got sick because he **wasn't wearing a hat**.
*on za-bo-LYEL, po-to-MU chto **SHAP-ku nye no-SIL**.*
Он заболел, потому что **шапку не носил**.

One hundred grams of vodka with pepper **will cure** anything.
*sto GRAM VOD-ki s PYER-tsem **VI-lye-chat** te-BYA ot vsye-VO.*
Сто грамм водки с перцем **вылечат** тебя от всего.

Someone must have **given me the evil eye**, because I've been getting sick a lot lately.
KTO-to na-VYER-no me-NYA SGLA-zil, po-to-MU chto v po-SLYEDnye-ye VRYE-mya ya CHAS-to bo-LYE-yu.
Кто-то наверное **меня сглазил**, потому что в последнее время я часто болею.

After I got the flu, my granny healed me with **mustard plasters**.
PO-sle to-VO, kak za-bo-LYEL GRI-ppom, mo-YA BAB-kaVI-lyechi-la me-NYA gor-CHICH-ni-ka-mi.
После того как заболел гриппом, моя бабка вылечила меня **горчичниками**.

Mustard plasters are still a popular way to treat respiratory illnesses in Russia.

I cured my stuffy nose by **inhaling potato vapors**.
ya svoi NAS-mork VI-lye-chil CHE-ryez vdi-KHA-ni-ye kar-TOfyel-no-vo PA-ra.
Я свой насморк вылечил через **вдыхание картофельного пара**.

I always treat a cold with **cupping**.
ya vseg-DA LYE-chu pro-STU-du BAN-ka-mi.
Я всегда лечу простуду **банками**.

If you've never heard of cupping, it basically involves lighting a match in little glass jars to create suction and then sticking them onto a sick person's back.

My aunt cured her cancer with **special herbal tea**.
mo-YA TYO-tya iz-le-CHI-la se-BYA ot RA-ka spye-tsi-AL-ni-mi cha-YA-mi na TRAV-kakh.
Моя тётя излечила себя от рака **специальными чаями на травках**.

I have a **fever**.
u me-NYA tyem-pye-ra-TU-ra.
У меня **температура**.

I'm **nauseous**.
me-NYA tosh-NIT.
Меня **тошнит**.

Do you have anything for **heartburn?**
u te-BYA YEST chto-ni-BUD ot iz-ZHO-gi?
У тебя есть что-нибудь от **изжоги**?

I can't think straight.
u me-NYA bash-KA nye VA-rit.
У меня башка не варит.

Do you need a **prescription** for these
antibiotics?
*NU-zhen li rye-TSEPT dlya E-tikh an-ti-bi-O-ti-
kov?*
Нужен ли **рецепт** для этих антибиотиков?
In Russia, the answer more often than not is no.

....

Sleep
son
Сон

If you ask me, the best thing to do for an illness is to sleep
it off. Note that the word сон in Russian means both "sleep"
and the kind of dream that you have when sleeping. There
is also another word for dream in Russian—мечта (*myech-
TA*)—but that's more like the kind of dream that Martin
Luther King Jr. had.

I'm tired as a dog.
ya u-STAL kak so-BA-ka.
Я устал как собака.

I'm worn out.
ya u-STAV-shii.
Я уставший.

I'm sleepy.
mnye KHO-chet-sya spat.
Мне хочется спать.

I want to take a nap.
kho-CHU po-drye-MAT.
Хочу **подремать**.

I'm on bed rest.
ya v SPAL-nom rye-ZHI-mye.
Я в спальном режиме.

It's time for me to go beddy-bye.
mnye po-RA SPAT-ki.
Мне пора спатки.

I just feel like lying around in bed today.
sye-VOD-nya KHO-chet-sya PRO-sto po-va-LYAT-sya v po-STYE-li.
Сегодня хочется просто **поваляться в постели**.

I overslept today.
ya sye-VOD-nya pro-SPAL.
Я сегодня **проспал**.

I'm gonna read a few more pages and then get some shut-eye.
ya pro-CHTU ye-SCHO PA-ru stra-NITS, a po-TOM MAssu po-da-VLYU.
Я прочту ещё пару страниц, а потом **массу подавлю**.

I usually watch TV before bed.
PYE-red snom ya o-BICH-no smo-TRYU TYE-lik.
Перед сном я обычно смотрю телик.

He snores like a pig.
on khra-PIT kak svi-NYA.
Он храпит как свинья.

I suffer from insomnia.
ya stra-DA-yu ot byes-SON-ni-tsi.
Я страдаю от **бессонницы**.

The Russian bathhouse
RUSS-ka-ya BA-nya
Русская баня

I love the *banya*. Hey, it's fun to hang out naked with your friends. And if you believe the Russians, steamin' it up in the bathhouse is one of the keys to good health, and being beaten with birch branches is a surefire way to release all of those toxins you've built up swilling vodka. Now who am I to argue with that?

Let's go for a steam!
da-VAI po-PA-rim-sya!
Давай попаримся!

Have a good steam!
s LYO-gkim PA-rom!
С лёгким паром!
This is what you say to someone on his way to the *banya*. If you've ever spent New Year's in Russia, you probably know this phrase from the classic Soviet film of the same name.

Let's leave our clothes in the **changing area.**
*da-VAI o-DYEZH-du o-STA-vim v **pryed-BA-nni-kye**.*
Давай одежду оставим в **предбаннике**.

Let's hit the **steam room.**
*poi-DYOM v **pa-RIL-ku**.*
Пойдём в **парилку**.

Hey, Vasya, could you **beat me with that branch** a little more?
*eh, VA-sya, ti MO-zhesh me-NYA ye-SCHO chut **po-PArit VYE-nich-kom**?*
Эй, Вася, ты можешь меня ещё чуть **попарить веничком**?
Vasya is a common Russian guy's name, but it is also sometimes used with random people in a sort of cheeky way.

Now that we've steamed up, let's go jump in the snow!
tye-PYER, kak kho-ro-SHO po-PA-ri-lis, poi-DYOM poPRI-ga-yem v snyeg!
Теперь, как хорошо попарились, пойдём попрыгаем в снег!
Steamin' it up is usually followed by a cold shower, a jump in a cold lake, or, in wintertime, a naked roll in the snow. It's all about the hot and cold contrasts.

I prefer white *banyas*.
*ya pryed-po-chi-TA-yu **BA-nyu po-BYEL-omu**.*
Я предпочитаю **баню по-белому**.
There are two basic types of *banya*: white *banya* (по-белому) and black *banya* (по-чёрному). White *banyas* are usually a bit better, as the smoke is vented through pipes. In black *banyas*, the smoke just goes through a hole in the ceiling.

He drank too much vodka and steamed himself to death.
on pye-rye-BRAL VOD-ku i za-PA-ril-sya.
Он перебрал водки и запарился.
Which does happen, apparently.

....

The crapper
sor-TIR
Сортир

Public restrooms are in short supply in Russia, and the ones that do exist are pretty rank. The most unfortunate type consists of a hole in the ground covered up by some rotting pieces of wood and covered with piss, shit, and those little squares of newspaper that people use for toilet paper. The better ones actually have a toilet, even if it's just some metal and porcelain contraption that you squat over. So if you need to answer nature's call while out and about in Russia, your best bet is probably to find a Mickey D's, where you can sit your ass down in relative luxury.

Yesterday, I spent all day sitting **on the potty.**
ya vchye-RA TSE-lii dyen si-DYEL na gor-SHKYE.
Я вчера целый день сидел **на горшке**.

I gotta go to **the toilet.**
mnye NA-do v uni-TAZ.
Мне надо **в унитаз**.

Where's the nearest **crapper?**
gdye SA-mii bli-ZHAI-ishii sor-TIR?
Где самый ближайший **сортир**?

That **shithole** is really nasty (both literally and figuratively).
E-ta pa-RA-sha SIL-no o-bo-SRA-nna-ya.
Эта **параша** сильно обосранная.
This is usually the word used for the holes in the ground that prisoners
crap in.

....

Urine
mo-CHA
моча

If you're a woman, the upside to the prevalence of the
Turkish toilet in Russia is that after a few months of
squatting over the piss hole, you'll have thighs you can
crack coconuts with.

When I drink beer, I have to **urinate** every five minutes.
*kog-DA ya PI-vo pyu, mnye NA-do mo-CHIT-sya KAZHdi-ye pyat
mi-NUT.*
Когда я пиво пью, мне надо **мочиться** каждые пять минут.

I think I need to **tinkle.**
po-MO-ye-ti mnye NA-do BRIZ-nut.
По-моему мне надо **брызнуть**.

I gotta **pee** bad.
mnye SROCH-no NA-do po-PI-sat.
Мне срочно надо **пописать**.
Watch your stress here. To pee is *PI-sat*. With the accent on the second syllable (*pi-SAT*), it means "to write."

I really gotta piss.
mnye O-chen NA-do pos-SAT.
Мне очень надо поссать.

I laughed so hard I wet myself.
ya tak sme-YAL-sya, chto o-bos-SAL-sya.
Я так смеялся, что обоссался.

....

Shit
gav-NO
Гавно

I think the most promising sign of Russia's economic upturn is the availability of white toilet paper. Don't get me wrong—you still likely won't find anything as squeezable as Charmin, but it sure beats the hell out of that stretchy brown crepe paper that used to pass for toilet paper back in the old days. Keep in mind that if you think you'll need to wipe your ass out in public, you might want to carry some with you, as most public restrooms lack this basic supply.

Where can I take a **dump**?
gdye tut MOZH-no po-SRAT?
Где тут можно **посрать**?

That **shit** really stinks.
E-to gov-NO FU kak vo-NYA-yet.
Это **говно** фу как воняет.

It smells like **crap** here.
tut PAKH-nyet dyer-MOM.
Тут пахнет **дерьмом**.

I have nasty **diarrhea**.
u me-NYA SIL-nii po-NOS.
У меня сильный **понос**.

After I ate at that shitty restaurant, I got **the runs**.
PO-sle to-VO, kak po-KU-shal v E-tom khrye-NO-vom resto-RA-nye,
u me-NYA po-ya-VI-las DRIS-nya.
После того, как покушал в этом хреновом ресторане, у меня
появилась **дрисня**.

I'm feeling a bit **constipated**.
u me-NYA chut za-POR.
У меня чуть **запор**.

Farting
PU-kan-i-ye
Пукание

Farting is no more publicly acceptable in Russia than it is in
the US. Fortunately, however, there is usually some stinking
drunk bum around that you can blame it on.

I'm a little **gassy**.
u me-NYA GA-zi-ki.
У меня **газики**.

He's a nasty **farter**.
on pro-TIV-nii VI-pyer-dish.
Он противный **выпердыш**.

He let out a **loud fart.**
on GROM-ko PUK-nul.
Он громко **пукнул**.

Hey, who **cut the cheese?**
eh, kto PYORD-nul?
Эй, кто **пёрднул**?

That one was **silent but deadly.**
E-to bil vo-NYU-chii bzdyekh.
Это был **вонючий бздех**.

Other bodily excretions
dru-GI-ye tye-LYES-ni-ye vi-dye-LYE-niya
Другие телесные выделения

One of the things that has always disgusted me about the provinces is the number of old men perfectly willing to blow snot rockets while hobbling along the street. I mean, I guess it's better than using your hand, but still, that's pretty nasty.

I gotta hurl.
mnye NA-do po-ri-GAT.
Мне надо порыгать.
Порыгать can also mean to blelch.

That moonshine made me lose my lunch.
ya po-ka-ZAL za-KUS-ku ot E-to-vo sa-mo-GO-na.
Я показал закуску от этого самогона.

Spit
SLYU-ni
Слюни

Snot
SOP-li
Сопли

> **Yuck! Don't blow your nose on your hand!**
> *Fuuu! Ne NA-do smor-KAT-sya v RU-ku!*
> Фууу! Не надо сморкаться в руку!

> **Stop picking your nose!**
> *KHVA-tit ko-vi-RYAT v no-SU!*
> Хватит ковырять в носу!

> **Gross! You got boogers hanging out of your nose!**
> *FU pro-TIV-no! u te-BYA iz NOs-a tor-CHAT ko- ZYAV-ki!*
> Фу противно! У тебя из носа торчат козявки!

Menstruation
myen-stru-A-tsi-ya
Менструация

> **I've got my period.**
> *u me-NYA MYE-syach-ni-ye.*
> У меня месячные.

> **Where can I buy some pads?**
> *gdye MOZH-no ku-PIT pro-KLAD-ki?*
> Где можно купить прокладки?

> **Do you have an extra tampon?**
> *YEST u te-BYA LISH-nii tam-PON?*
> Есть у тебя лишний тампон?

CHAPTER 5

Nice & Naughty
DO-brii i GAD-kii
Добрый и Гадкий

There used to be a saying that there was no sex in the Soviet Union. Well, Russians have come a long way since then and, like those in many European cultures, now make Americans look like the puritanical prudes who founded our country.

Screwing
TRA-kha-nie
Траханье

Let's ...
da-VAI ...
Давай ...

> **have some sex**
> *po-za-ni-MA-yem-sya SYEKS-som*
> позанимаемся сексом

> **make love**
> *po-za-ni-MA-yem-sya liu-BO-viu*
> позанимаемся любовью

screw
po-TRA-kha-yem-sya
Потрахаемся

fuck
po-ye-BYOM-sya
поебёмся

bang
po-FAK-a-yem-sya
пофакаемся
From the English verb "to fuck."

roll in the hay
VYA-lo-vo po-PA-rit
вялого попарить

We screwed all night.
mi TRA-kha-lis vsyu noch.
Мы трахались всю ночь.

Fuck me!
ye-BI me-NYA!
Еби меня!

I usually have sex about three times a week.
ya o-BICH-no za-ni-MA-yus SEKS-om RA-za tri v nyeDYE-lyu.
Я обычно занимаюсь сексом раза три в неделю.

I really need a good screw.
mnye O-chen NA-do kho-RO-shu-yu SHVOR-ku.
Мне очень надо хорошую шворку.

From the moment we met, I've wanted to **nail her**.
*c mo-MYEN-ta zna-KOM-stva, ya tak kho-CHU yei **PALku KI-nut**.*
С момента знакомства, я так хочу ей **палку кинуть**.

He gave me a really **good lay**.
*on me-NYA **na-YA-ri-val na vo-lo-SYAN-kye**.*
Он меня **наяривал на волосянке**.

SUCK MY...
OT-SO-SI MOI...
ОТСОСИ МОЙ...

All of these requests—with the exception of "spank"—will be followed by a noun in the accusative case.

Lick my...
ob-LI-zi-vai moi/mo-YU...
Облизывай мой/мою...

Kiss my...
po-tse-LUI moi/mo-YU...
Поцелуй мой/мою...

Tickle my...
po-sche-ko-CHI moi/mo-YU...
Пощекочимой/мою...

Touch my...
TRO-gai moi/mo-YU...
трогай мой/мою...

Feel my...
po-SHU-pai moi/mo-YU...
Пощупай мой/мою...

Grope my...
MA-tsai moi/mo-YU...
Мацай мой/мою...

Bite my...
y-ku-SI moi/mo-YU...
Укуси мой/мою...

Spank my...
po-KHLO-pai mnye po...
Похлопай мне по (plus dative)...

Massage my...
mas-sa-ZHI-rui moi/mo-YU...
массажируй мой/мою...

I'm really **turned on** by chicks wearing **ass floss.**
*me-NYA tak **voz-buzh-DA-yut** DYEV-ki v **zho-po-RYE-zakh.***
Меня так **возбуждают** девки в **жопорезах**.

Let's have a quickie.
da-VAI po BIS-tro-mu.
Давай по быстрому.

More! More!
ye-SCHO! ye-SCHO!
Ещё! Ещё!

Ouch! Watch out for my pubes!
oy! Ak-ku-RAT-no s vo-lo-SYAN-koi!
Ой! Аккуратно с волосянкой!

Please be gentle, I'm a virgin.
NYEZH-no, po-ZHA-lui-sta, ya DYEV-stvyen-nik/DYEV-stvyen-ni-tsa.
Нежно, пожалуйста, я **Девственник/девственница.**
If you're one of those guys who's come to Russia thinking you'll find some hot young virgin to marry, you will probably be disappointed. While she may be hot and she may be young, chances are if she tells you she's a virgin, she is either lying or under 14.

Ass
ZHO-pa
Жопа

There's nothing like a big ol' butt.

Stick it in my....
vstav mnye v ...
Вставь мне в ...

Let's do it in the....
da-VAI v ...
Давай в ...
The following are all in the accusative.

> **butt**
> *PO-pu*
> попу

> **booty**
> *an-ti-FEIS*
> антифейс
> Get it? Anti-face.

backdoor
och-KO
очко

bum
GUZ-no
гузно

bumper
BAM-per
бампер

bottom
ZAD-ni-tsu
задницу

Dick
khui
Хуй

Most Russian men are uncut, the way nature made them. And like men all around the world, they have a large range of pet names for their little friend in their pants.

Suck my....
ot-so-SI moi....
Отсоси мой....

Jerk off my....
dro-CHI moi....
Дрочи мой....
All of the following terms will be in the acusative.

member
chlyen
член

BLOW JOBS
MI-NYE-TI
МИНЕТЫ

I could really use a blow job.
mnye bi NA-do mi-NYET.
Мне бы надо минет.

Blow me!
ot-so-SI u me-NYA!
Отсоси у меня!

Gimme some head!
SDYE-lai mnye ot-SOS!
Сделай мне отсос!

Come on, **smoke my pipe.**
da-VAI ku-RI mo-YU TRUB-ku.
Давай **кури мою трубку**.

She's really a pro at **playing the skin flute.**
o-NA MAS-ter po i-GRYE na KO-zha-noi FLEIT-ye.
Она мастер по **игре на кожаной флейте**.

Wanna suck my **lollipop?**
khoch po-so-SAT mo-YU kon-FYET-ku?
Хочь пососать мою **конфектку?**

I wanna **cum** in your mouth.
ya kho-CHU KON-chit v rot.
Я хочу **кончить** в рот.

I've never blown an **uncut dick** before!
ya ni-kog-DA nye ot-SA-si-va-la nye-ob-RYE-zan-nii khui!
Я никогда не отсасывала **необрезанный хуй**!

cock
khryen
хрен

johnson
kher
хер

pee pee (the body part, not the liquid that comes out of it)
PIS-ku
письку
This can refer to both male and female genitalia.

sausage
kol-BA-si-nu
колбасину

little prick
khu-ISH-ko
хуишко

....

Balls
YAI-tsa
Яйца

She fucked me so hard, my **nuts** hurt.
o-NA tak SIL-no me-NYA ye-BLA, chto bo-LYE-li mo-I YO-bal-di.
Она так сильно меня ебла, что болели мои **ёбалды**.

Do my **marbles** seem too big to you?
mo-I ko-lo-KOL-chi-ki te-BYE nye KA-zhut-sa SLISHkom bol-SHI-ye?
Мои **колокольчики** тебе не кажутся слишком большие?

I pissed her off, so she kicked me in the **nads**.
ya ye-YO ra-zo-ZLIL, i o-NA da-LA mnye v ak-ku-muLYA-to-ri.
Я её разозлил, и она дала мне в **аккумуляторы**.

I love when she licks my **junk**.
ya liu-BLYU kog-DA o-NA ob-LI-zi-va-yet moi pri-BOR.
Я люблю когда она облизывает мой **прибор**.

I have a weird pain in my **balls.**
u men-YA STRA-na-ya bol v mud-YE.
У меня странная боль в **муде**.

....

Tits
SI-ski
Сиськи

If you're a guy, I suppose one of the perks of being in Russia is that you will likely see an exceptional number of tits. There seems to be no short supply of young, braless women in skimpy shirts who turn all of Russia into one big wet T-shirt contest with the first rains of spring.

Squeeze my....
TIS-kai mnye....
Тискай мне ...

Pinch my....
po-shi-PAI mnye....
Пощипай мне ...

> **breasts**
> *GRU-di*
> груди
>
> **tits**
> *SI-ski*
> сиськи
>
> **titties**
> *TIT-ki*
> титьки

melons
BUL-ki
булки

I have the biggest **tits** out of all my friends.
u me-NYA SA-mi-ye bol-SHI-ye SIS-ki sre-DI svo-IKH po-DRUG.
У меня самые большие **сиськи** среди своих подруг.

I prefer tiny **titties**.
ya pryed-po-chi-TA-yu ma-LYU-syen-ki-ye TIT-ki.
Я предпочитаю малюсенькие **титьки**.

When I took off her bra, her **knockers** just about hit me in the face.
kog-DA ya snyal ye-YO LIF-chik, ye-YO bu-fe-RA chut ne u-DA-ri-li mnye v li-TSO.
Когда я снял её лифчик, её **буфера** чуть не ударили мне в лицо.

....

Pussy
piz-DA
Пизда

Lick my....
po-li-ZHI mnye....
Полижи мне ...
The following are all in the accusative case.

vagina
vla-GA-li-sche
влагалище

muff
MAN-du
манду

cunt
schyel
щель

snatch
piz-DYON-ka
пиздёнка

shaved pussy
pye-LOT-ka BRI-ta-ya
пелотка бритая

unshaved pussy
pye-LOT-ka nye-BRI-ta-ya
пелотка небритая

clitoris
KLI-tor
клитор

clit
SI-kyel
сикель

The inner thigh cream pie
myezh-du-NOZH-no-ye pi-RO-zhe-no-ye
Междуножное пирожное

Damn, she has a forest down there!
blin, u nye-YO lyes tam ras-TYOT!
Блин, у нё лес там растёт!

I'm completely shaved.
ya POL-nost-yu BRI-ta-ya.
Я полностью бритая.

Sex positions and perversions
syek-su-AL-ni-ye po-ZI-tsii i iz-vra-SCHEni-ya
Сексуальные позиции и извращения

Sex in Russia is rapidly becoming more adventurous, bypassing the standard missionary position of days gone by. There is little taboo attached to watching the occasional skin flick, and women often seem to enjoy them even more than the guys. So make some popcorn, pop in some porn, and get your groove on.

Missionary
mis-si-o-NYER-ska-ya
Миссионерская

Guy on top
muzh-CHI-na SVYER-khu
Мужчина сверху

Girl on top
ZHEN-shi-na SVYER-khu
Женщина сверху

Legs in the air
GU-sar-ska-ya
Гусарская

Spoon position
PO-za SBO-ku
Поза сбоку
Also called ложечка (*LO-zhech-ka*).

69
shest-dye-SYAT DYE-vyat
Шестьдесят девять

FIFTY SHADES OF GRAY
PYS-DYE-SYAT OT-TYEN-KOV SYER-O-VO
ПЯТЬДЕСЯТ ОТТЕНКОВ СЕРОГО

In Russian, BDSM is also called БДСМ (*be-de-es-em*) which is broken down to Бондаж/Дисциплина (*BON-dazh/dis-tsi-PLIN-a*/Bondage & Discipline) and Садизм/мазохизм (*sa-DIZ-m/ma-so-KHIZ-m*/Sadism & Masochism). Another important acronym to know if you feel like getting your freak on is БРД, the equivalent of SSC (Safe, Sane, Consensual), which stands for Безопасность, Разумность, Добровольность (*bez-o-PAS-nost, raz-UM-nost, do-bro-VOL-nost*), which is what you should be keeping it.

Give me a golden shower.
SDYE-lai mnye zo-lo-TOI dozhd.
Сделай мне **золотой дождь**.

I'm into anal sex.
ya ta-SCHUS ot a-NAL-no-vo SYEK-sa.
Я тащусь от анального секса.

Let's take a trip from Istan-blow to Butt-apest.
da-VAI po-pu-tye-SHEST-vu-yem iz rot-ter-DA-ma v popyen-GA-gyen.
Давай попутешествуем из Роттердама в Попенгаген.
This means oral sex followed by anal sex. It is based on a pun on the words for "mouth" (рот) and "butt" (попа) and the city names Rotterdam and Copenhagen. This is kinda prison slangy—normal people don't really say it, but I think it's hilarious.

I wanna have a threesome with you and your sister.
ya kho-CHU syeks vtro-YOM s to-BOI i s tvo-YEI syes-TROI.
Я хочу **секс втроём** с тобой и с твоей сестрой.

Ménage à trois

SHVYED-ska-ya sye-MYA

Шведская семья

Literally, a "Swedish family," which kinda makes me wonder what the hell is going on in Sweden. There is also the term полиамория/*po-li-a-MOR-i-ya* (polyamory).

Let's have an orgy.

da-VAI u-STRO-im OR-gi-yu.

Давай устроим оргию.

Group sex

Ggup-po-VU-kha

Групповуха

Other words you might hear meaning group sex include цирк (*tsirk*), эстафета (*es-ta-FYE-ta*), and карусель (*ka-ru-SYEL*).

Let's watch some porn.

da-VAI po-SMO-trim por-NU-khu.

Давай посмотрим порнуху.

My turn-ons include big tits, midgets, and whipped cream.

me-NYA voz-bu-ZHDA-yut bol-SHI-ye SIS-ki, KAR-li-ki, i VZBI-ti-ye SLIV-ki.

Меня возбуждают большие сиськи, карлики, и взбитые сливки.

I'm into....

ya u-vlye-KA-yus....

Я увлекаюсь....

Note that this phrase takes the instrumental case.

bondage

BON-dazh-om

бондажом

sadomasochism

sa-do-ma-zo-KHIZ-mom

садомазохизмом

discipline
dis-tsi-PLIN-oi
дисциплиной

fetishism
fe-ti-SHIZ-mom
фетишизмом

submission
pod-chi-NYE-nyem
подчинением

sadism
sa-DIZ-mom
садизмом

masochism
ma-zo-KHIZ-mom
мазохизмом

spanking
SPAN-kin-gom
спанкингом

fisting
FIS-tin-gom
фистингом

flagellation
fla-gyel-LYA-tsiye
флагелляцией

role play
ro-lye-VY-mi IG-ra-mi
ролевыми играми

age play
i-GROY s pod-MYEN-oy VOZ-ras-ta
игрой с подменой возраста

gender play
i-GROY s pod-MYEN-oy PO-la
игрой с подменой пола

body modification
mo-di-fi-KA-tsi-ye TYE-la
модификацией тела

piercing
PIR-sin-gom
пирсингом

branding
BREN-din-gom
брэндингом

Sorry, I'm **vanilla**.
iz-vi-NI, no ya va-NIL.
Извини, но я **ваниль.**

I make my **slave** wear a **collar**.
ya za-sta-VLYA-yu, SHTO-by moy rab no-SIL o-SHEY-nik.
Я заставляю, чтобы мой **раб** носил **ошейник.**

Fuck, I forget the **safe word**.
BLYAD, ya za-BIL stop-SLO-vo.
Блядь, я забыл **стоп-слово.**

I heard about a new sex club that has a real **dungeon**.
ya SLI-shal pro NO-vii SYEKS klub, gdye na-sto-YA-shch-ya TYEM-ni-tsa.
Я слышал про новый секс клуб, где настоящая **темница.**

He's a businessman by day and a **dungeon master** by night.
DNYOM on biz-nyes-MEN a NO-chyu nad-zi-RA-tel.
Днём он бизнесмен а ночью **надзиратель.**

I'm a (female) **sub** in need of a (male) **dom**.
Ya SA-ba, ko-TOR-a-ya nuzh-DA-yet-sa v DOM-ye.
Я **саба**, которая нуждается в **доме.**

I'm a (male) **sub** in need of a (female) **dom**.
*ya **sab**, ko-TOR-ii nuzh-DA-yet-sa v **do-MIN-ye**.*
Я **саб**, который нуждается в **домине**.

I'm looking for a **dominatrix** who will whip me.
*ya i-SHCHU **do-mi-NA-trik-sa**, ko-TOR-a-ya BU-dyet khlye-STAT
MYE-nya.*
Я ищу **доминатрикса**, которая будет хлестать меня.

Got any **handcuffs**?
*YEST u te-BYA **na-RUCH-ni-ki**?*
Есть у тебя **наручники**?

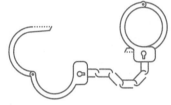

Orgasm
or-GAZM
Оргазм

I'm cumming!
ya kon-CHA-yu!
Я кончаю!

You got cum all over my leg!
ti pro-LIL kon-CHI-nu na mo-YU NO-gu!
Ты пролил кончину на мою ногу!

Cum on my face!
KON-chi na mo-YO li-TSO!
Кончи на моё лицо!

He **jizzed** all over my bed!
*on **za-va-FLIL** mnye vsyu pos-TYEL!*
Он **завафлил** мне всю постель!

I've never seen so much **semen** in all my life!
*ya ni-kog-DA v ZHIZ-ni nye VI-dye-la STOL-ko **SPYER-mi**!*
Я никогда в жизни не видела столько **спермы**!

Wow, I've never seen a **female ejaculation** before!
*UKH ti, ya ni-kog-DA RAN-she nye VI-dyel **ZHEN-sku-yu e-YA-ku-lya-tsi-yu**!*
Ух ты, я никогда раньше не видел **женскую эякуляцию**!

Holy shit, **multiple orgasms**!
YOB, E-to MNO-zhest-vye-nnii or-GAZM!
Ёб, это **множественный оргазм**!

....

Sluts and fuck buddies
BLYA-di i ye-bu-NI
Бляди и ебуны

Sometimes you're just looking for a good time. No shame in that.

You are such a **temptress**!
*ti ta-KA-ya **so-blaz-NI-tyel-nitsa**!*
Ты такая **соблазнительница**!

I'm only looking for a **fuck buddy**.
*ya i-SCHU lish **ye-bu-NA**.*
Я ищу лишь **ебуна**.

He cheated on me with some **slut**.
*on mnye iz-mye-NIL s ka-KOI-to **SHLU-khoi**.*
Он мне изменил с какой-то **шлюхой**.

She found out that he's been **stepping out**.
*o-NA uz-NA-la, shto on **i-DYOT na LYE-vo**.*
Она узнала, что он **идёт на лево**.

She's an easy lay.
o-NA lyog-KA-ya na pye-rye-DOK.
Она лёгкая на передок.

He/She is only into **one-night stands**.
on/o-NA TOL-ko LYU-bit syeks na od-NU noch.
Он/Она только любит **секс на одну ночь**.

She smacked me in the face when I called her a **sleazy cunt**.
o-NA da-LA mnye po-SCHO-chi-nu, kog-DA ya ye-YO naz-VAL piz-DOI s u-SHA-mi.
Она дала мне пощёчину, когда я её назвал **пиздой с ушами**.

My neighbor is a disgusting **Peeping Tom**.
moi so-SYED pro-TIV-nii so-blya-da-TAI.
Мой сосед противный **соблядатай**.

He's a **male slut**.
on blya-DUN.
Он **блядун**.

He's a total **horn dog**.
u nye-VO piz-do-ma-NI-ya.
У него **пиздомания**.

Man, that old guy in my building is such a **pervert**.
blin, E-tot sta-RIK v mo-YOM DO-mye ta-KOI iz-vraSCHE-nyets.
Блин, этот старик в моём доме такой **извращенец**.

She found herself a new **lover (male)** at the disco.
o-NA na-SHLA se-BYE NO-vo-vo KHA-kha-lya na disko-TYE-kye.
Она нашла себе нового **хахаля** на дискотеке.

Are all Russian jokes about women who **whore around** while their husbands are on business trips?
nye-u-ZHELI vsye RU-sski-ye a-nek-DO-ti o TOM, kak ZHEN-schi-ni blya-DU-yut kog-DA svo-I MU-zhya v koman-di-ROV-kye?
Неужели все русские анекдоты о том, как женщины **блядуют** когда свои мужья в командировке?

I went to a nightclub looking for some **cheap meat**.
ya po-SHOL v noch-NOI klub v POI-skakh ras-kla- DU-shki.
Я пошёл в ночной клуб в поисках **раскладушки**.

Masturbation

o-na-NIZM

Онанизм

If all else fails, it may be time to spank the ol' monkey. It's safe, it's cheap, and it won't expect you to pay for dinner.

I think I'm just going to sit home tonight and **jack off.**
na-VYER-no ya se-VOD-nya PRO-sto po-si-ZHU DO-ma i po-dro-CHU.
Наверно я сегодня просто посижу дома и **подрочу**.

When I can't find a girl, I just **choke the chicken.**
YES-li nye mo-GU nai-TI dyev-CHON-ku, ya PRO-sto LIso-vo v ku-la-KYE go-NYU.
Если не могу найти девчонку, я просто **лысого в кулаке гоню**.

Every night, I like to watch some porn and **tune the violin.**
KAZH-dii VYE-cher ya lyu-BLYU smo-TRYET por-NU-khu i na-STRA-i-vat SKRIP-ku.
Каждый вечер я люблю смотреть порнуху и **настраивать скрипку**.

What the hell do I need men for when I can get off with a **vibrator?**
ka-KO-vo KHRYEna mnye NA-do muzh-CHI-nu, kogDA ya kai-FU-yu ot vi-BRA-to-ra?
Какого хрена мне надо мужчину, когда я кайфую от **вибратора**?

That **bean flipper** just wants a new **electric vibrator** for her birthday.
E-ta ba-la-LAI-ka TOL-ko KHO-chet NO-vii e-lek-troSHTU-tser na svoi dyen rozh-DYE-ni-ya.
Эта **балалайка** только хочет новый **электроштуцер** на свой день рождения.

Prostitution

pro-sti-TU-tsi-ya
Проституция

If you're striking out, don't lose hope. As long as the provinces remain poor and the Ukrainian border stays open, whores in Russia will be plentiful and cheap. So where does one find a good whore in Russia? I'm glad you asked! There are tons of cruising strips (called *tochki*), brothels (*bordeli*), classified ads in expat newspapers, and high-end nightclubs and strip joints that can hook you up. It's likely that your own hotel will even have an in-house supply, all of whom are ready, willing, and able to fulfill your every sick and twisted fantasy for a few greenbacks. If all else fails, just ask a cab driver where you can find a girl, and for a few extra bucks he will take you to the place. Here are some words you'll need to know to be a satisfied John.

Where can I find a...?
gdye MOZH-no na-i-TI...?
Где можно найти…?
These are all in the accusative.

> **prostitute**
> *pro-sti-TUT-ku*
> проститутку
>
> **hooker**
> *noch-NU-yu BA-boch-ku*
> ночную бабочку
>
> **whore**
> *SHLYU-khu*
> шлюху

trick
shar-MU-tu
шармуту

slut
po-tas-KU-khu
потаскуху

streetwalker
U-lich-nu-yu FYE-yu
уличную фею

Where's the nearest **cruising strip?**
gdye SA-ma-ya bli-ZHAI-sha-ya TOCH-ka?
Где самая ближайшая **точка**?

Sometimes also called a панель (*pa-NYEL*).

Pimp
su-te-NYOR
Сутенёр
When it comes to street prostitution, most of the pimps are part of either Chechen or Dagestani mafia groups, and they are some serious mofos. Don't fuck with them.

John
cha-sov-SCHIK
Часовщик
Specifically one who pays by the hour.

Brothel
bor-DYEL
Бордель

Do you know a good **whorehouse** in Moscow?
ti nye ZNA-yesh kho-RO-shii tra-kho-DROM vmosk-VYE?
Ты не знаешь хороший **траходром** в Москве?

Hey, I ordered a blonde!
eh, a za-ka-ZAL blon-DIN-ku!
Ей, я заказал блондинку!

Contraceptives

pro-ti-vo-za-CHA-toch-ni-ye SRYED-stva

Противозачаточные средства

There is a Russian saying that goes, "having sex with a condom is like smelling flowers through a gas mask." While not all Russian men are that categorical—or poetic—when it comes to birth control, there can still be a lot of resistance. Nevertheless, condoms of varied quality, color, and expiration date are widely available throughout Russia, as are various spermicidal suppositories (called свечи, *svechi*) and other nasty things you would probably never want to touch with your hands, much less any other part of your anatomy. Abortion, however, is still the main form of birth control, especially in the provinces.

Have you got a...?

YEST u te-BYA...?

Есть у тебя…?

> **condom**
>
> *prye-zyer-va-TIV*
>
> презерватив

> **johnny**
>
> *gon-DON*
>
> гондон
>
> When this word refers to a person, it means something more along the lines of "total douchebag."

> **rubber**
>
> *ga-LO-sha*
>
> галоша

raincoat
pa-ra-SHUT
парашют

dick shield
na-KHUI-nik
нахуйник

Don't worry, I'm on the pill.
nye pye-rye-zhi-VAI, ya ta-BLYET-ki pyu.
Не переживай, я таблетки пью.

....

Pregnancy
bye-RYE-mye-nnost
Беременность

I'm late.
u me-NYA za-DYER-zhka.
У меня задержка.

She's expecting.
o-NA v po-lo-ZHE-nii.
Она в положении.

Honey, I'm **pregnant** with another man's baby.
*do-ro-GOI, ya **bye-RYE-mye-nna** ot dru-GO-vo muzhCHI-ni.*
Дорогой, я **беременна** от другого мужчины.

He dumped her as soon as she got **knocked up.**
*on ye-YO BRO-sil, kak TOL-ko o-NA **za-lye-TYE-la.***
Он её бросил, как только она **залетела.**

She's had five **abortions** already and is probably **sterile** now.
*o-NA u-ZHE SDYE-la-la pyat **a-BOR-tov** i na-VYER-no tye-PYER **byes-PLOD-na-ya.***
Она уже сделала пять **абортов** и наверно теперь **бесплодная.**

STDs
be-pe-pe-PE
БППП

БППП stands for Болезни, передаваемые половым путем (*bo-LYEZ-ni, pye-rye-da-VA-ye-mi-ye po-lo-VIM pu-TYOM*), or sexually transmitted diseases. There are a lot of STDs floating around Russia, but that's not the scary part. The scary part is the astronomical rate at which HIV has spread in Russia, now infecting well over a million people. It used to be restricted almost entirely to IV drug users and prostitutes, but over the years it has started to seep into the general population. The thing is, testing isn't very common, and many Russians are turned off by condoms, so there are a lot of people walking around who have no idea that they are infected. As for treatment, don't even ask. Even if good treatment were available, most Russians can't afford it. All in all, it is a tragedy still unfolding, and one that many Russians deny even exists.

I **caught an STD** from that bitch I was dating.
*ya **poi-MAL na KON-chik** ot E-toi SU-ki, s ko-TO-roi ya vstrye-CHAL-sya.*
Я **поймал на кончик** от этой суки, с которой я встречался.

That bastard gave me **crabs**!
*E-ta SVO-loch pye-rye-DAL mnye **man-da-VOSH-ku**!*
Эта сволочь передал мне **мандавошку**!

It hurts when I piss—I think I have **the clap** again.
*bo-LIT, kog-DA ya PI-sa-yu—po-MO-ye-mu u me-NYA o-PYAT **gu-SAR-skii NAS-mork**.*
Болит, когда я писаю—по-моему у меня опять **гусарский насморк**.

I got a strange rash on my dick—I hope it's not **herpes**.
u me-NYA STRA-nna-ya sip na khu-YE—na-DYE-yus, E-to nye GYER-pyes.
У меня странная сыпь на хуе—надеюсь, это не **герпес**.

Do you need a prescription for **penicillin** in Russia?
NU-zhen li rye-TSEPT dlya pye-ni-tsi-LLI-na v ro-SSII?
Нужен ли рецепт для **пенициллина** в России?

Where can I find a doctor who treats **venereal disease**?
gdye MOZH-no na-i-TI vra-CHA, ko-TO-rii LYE-chit vyenye-RI-ches-ki-ye bo-LYEZ-ni?
Где можно найти врача, который лечит **венерические болезни**?

I heard he's HIV infected.
ya SLI-shal, chto on vich-in-fi-TSI-ro-van.
Я слышал, что он ВИЧ – инфицирован.

He was sick for a long time, and they finally discovered he had **AIDS**.
on DOL-go bo-LYEL i na-ko-NYETS ob-na-RU-zhi-li, chto u nye-VO spid.
Он долго болел и наконец обнаружили, что у него **СПИД**.

CHAPTER 6

Smack Talk
go-vo-RIT GA-dost
Говорить Гадость

If you spend even a short amount of time in Russia, sooner or later someone is gonna piss you off. Choose your words carefully though, as alcohol + pissed-off Russian = a situation that could escalate unexpectedly fast. If you're ready to put your money where your mouth is and you're crazy enough to see it through to the bitter end, here you go. Udachi!

Get outta my face!
s glaz do-LOI!
С глаз долой!

You talkin' to me?
ti MNYE go-vo-RISH?
Ты мне говоришь?

Hey, buddy, what's the problem?
eh, dru-ZHOK, chto za pro-BLYE-ma?
Эй, дружок, что за проблема?

What's the deal?
v chom DYE-lo?
В чём дело?

Why are you messing with me?
cho ti pri-sta-YOSH?
Чё ты пристаёшь?

What the hell is going on here?
chto za BLYAD-stvo?
Что за блядство?

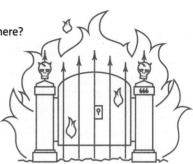

What is this mess?
chto za bar-DAK?
Что за бардак?

What is this nonsense?
cho E-to za bai-DA?
Чё это за байда?

Stop your frontin'!
nye vi-PYEN-dri-vaj-sya!
Не выпендривайся!

What, have you lost your mind?
u tebya CHTO, KRI-sha po-YE-kha-la?
У тебя что, крыша поехала?

What the hell do you want, you little shit?
CHO tye NA-do, gav-NYUK?
Чё те надо, гавнюк?

Piss off!
i-DI ti NA fig!
Иди ты на фиг!

Shove off!
po-SHOL ti!
Пошёл ты!

I've had it up to here with you!
ya to-BOI sit po GOR-lo!
Я тобой сыт по горло!

Go to hell!
i-DI k CHOR-tu!
Иди к чёрту!

I've run out of patience already!
u-ZHE LOP-nu-la mo-YO tyer-PYE-niye!
Уже лопнуло моё терпение!

I've fucking had it with you!
ti me-NYA za-ye-BAL!
Ты меня заебал!

I'm sick of your stupid mug!
mnye na-do-YE-la tvo-YA du-RATS-ka-ya RO-zha!
Мне надоела твоя дурацкая рожа!

Why are you draining me like this?
cho ti KROV iz mye-NYA vi-SA-si-VA-yesh?
Чё ты кровь из меня высасываешь?

You make me sick!
ti mnye na-do-YEL do tosh-no-TI!
Ты мне надоел до тошноты!

Get outta here, bitch!
va-LI ot-SYU-da, SU-ka!
Вали отсюда, сука!

Get your sorry ass outta here!
che-SHI BUL-ka-mi ot-SYU-da!
Чеши булками отсюда!

Get the fuck away from me!
ot-ye-BIS ot me-NYA!
Отъебись от меня!

Get your hands off me!
RU-ki PROCH ot me-NYA!
Руки прочь от меня!

Leave me alone!
o-STAV me-NYA v po-KO-ye!
Оставь меня в покое!

Move your ass!
PIZ-dui!
Пиздуй!

I don't have time for you!
mnye nye do te-BYA sei-CHAS!
Мне не до тебя сейчас!

Don't even think you can **dis me** like that.
DA-zhe nye DU-mai, chto MO-zhesh me-NYA khui nye STA-vit.
Даже не думай, что можешь **меня в хуй не ставить**.

Don't try to **screw me over**.
nye sta-RAI-sya me-NYA vyer-TYET na ba-NA-nye.
Не старайся меня **вертеть на банане**.

DAMN!
CHORT!
ЧЁРТ!

Darn!	*blin!*	Блин!
Damn!	*blyad!*	Блядь!
Dammit!	*BLA-kha MU-kha!*	Бляха муха!
Oh, snap!	*YO mo-YO!*	Ё моё!
Goddammit!	*chort voz-MI!*	Чёрт возьми!
Well, shoot!	*YOL-ki PAL-ki!*	Ёлки палки!
Fucking shit!	*ye-BA-tsa-SRA-tsa!*	Ебаться-сраться!
Fuck!	*piz-DYETZ!*	Пиздец
Fuckin' A!	*ye-BAT ko-PAT*	Ебать - копать!

Don't play me for an idiot!
nye DYEL-ai iz me-NYA i-di-O-ta!
Не делай из меня идиота!

What, are you trying to **rip me off?**
*ti CHO, KHO-chesh **ob-o-DRAT** me-NYA kak LI-pu?*
Ты чё, хочешь **ободрать меня как липу**?

If you touch me again, my husband's **gonna kick your ass.**
*YES-li ye-SCHO raz me-NYA TRO-nyesh, muzh **te-BYE piz-dyu-LEI na-VYE-sha-yet**.*
Если ещё раз меня тронешь, муж **тебе пиздюлей навешает**.

Stop giving me the third!
KHVA-tit me-NYA mu-RI-zhit!
Хватит меня мурыжить!

Don't screw around!
nye BA-lui-sya!
Не балуйся!

Quit BSing me!
nye ras-SKA-zi-vai mnye BAI-ki!
Не рассказывай мне байки!

Fuck off!
po-SHOL NA khui!
Пошёл на хуй!

This is the most common way to tell someone to fuck off. Keep in mind that the form has to change if you're talking to a girl (пошла на хуй!/ *po-SHLA NA khui*) or to a group of people (пошли на хуй!/ *po-SHLI NA khui*). Although this one phrase will always take you where you wanna go, if you like a little variety in your cursing, here are some other phrases you can use with more or less the same general meaning.

Fuck your mother!
YOB tvo-YU mat!
Ёб твою мать!

Fuck no!
khui v rot!
Хуй в рот!

What the fuck!
na khu-YU VI-dyet!
На хую видеть!

Blow me!
ot-so-SI mye-NYA!
Отсоси меня!

F you!
po-SHOL na tri BUK-vi!
Пошёл на три буквы!

While most Russians do understand the gesture of giving the bird, they also have a gesture called the фиг (*fig*), which is used in the same way but is formed by making a fist and putting your thumb between your index and middle finger. For example:

> **He gave me the fig.**
> *on dal mnye fig.*
> Он дал мне фиг.
>
> In other words, "he flipped me off, Russian style." Another way of saying this is Он показал мне шиш (*on po-ka-ZAL mnye SHISH*).

Go fuck yourself!
i-DI v ZHO-pu!
Иди в жопу!
Literally, "go to ass."

What the hell for?
na koy CHYORT?
На кой чёрт?

No way in hell!
CHYOR-ta s dva!
Чёрта с два!

Fuck you in the mouth!
ye-BAT te-BYA v rot!
Ебать тебя в рот!

....

Putin is a dickhead
PU-tin khuy-LO
Путин Хуйло

"Putin Khuilo" started out as a soccer chant around the time the Russian Army began its annexation of Crimea. It quickly went ridiculously viral with many—like, a bajillion—memes appearing on Facebook. And then there were the musical interpretations, the mariachi version being a personal favorite. The joke has gotten a bit tired, but it still makes the rounds, culminating in some Ukrainian astronomers recently paying to have a star named Putin Huilo. So the next time you gaze up at the night sky, remember: Putin is a dickhead. In addition, a whole lotta slang words were created to creatively express the growing animosity between Ukrainians, Russians, and Russian-loving Ukrainians.

Banderovets
ban-DER-o-vyets
Бандеровец
This comes from the name of a controversial Ukrainian partisan leader during WWII, Stepan Bandera. If you ask the Russians, he was a fascist and a Nazi-collaborator, but to Ukrainian nationalists, he is a national hero who fought against Soviet occupation of Ukraine. The term Бандеровец also has this dual meaning: When a Russian uses it, it

usually means something like "Ukrainian fascist." When a Ukrainian uses it, it's more an indication of (anti-Russian) Ukrainian patriotism.

Maidown
Майдаун

This combines the words Maidan and Down, as in Down's Syndrome. Remember all those Ukrainians who camped out on the main square of Kiev, called Madain? Well, if you consider them stupid, you'd call them майдауны.

Ukrop
Укроп

This word literally means "dill," and so the symbol of those who call themselves укропы is often dill leaves. In the context of politics, however, it refers to Ukrainian patriots.

Democrap
der-mo-KRAT
Дерьмократ

This combines the words дерьмо (*der-MO*, or crap) демократ (de-mo-KRAT, or democrat). Obviously, it is a not a compliment to those who advocate supposedly democratic positions.

Vatnik/Vatan
Ватник/Ватан

This is from another meme gone wild. A vatnik basically refers to a Russian who is not too bright and who loves him some Putin.

Putler
Путлер

This is a combination of Путин (Putin) and Гитлер (Hitler). Because Putin is not a very nice guy. You'll sometimes see it in graffiti, such as "Путлер Капут" (Putler Kaput).

Krimnashist
Крымнашист

So remember when Russia annexed Crimea? Russians lost their minds and started yelling "Крым наш! (*krim NASH!!*/Crimea is ours!)" every time a TV camera was pointed at them. From that phrase comes the term "krimnashists," referring to those Russians who saw the annexation as the long overdue return of a land that rightfully belongs to them (though they conveniently forgot not only about Ukrainian sovereignty, but also about the native population of Crimean Tatars who have inhabited the land for centuries).

Then there are those poor Russophile Ukrainians. It seems everyone despises them: Russians look down on them because they're Ukrainian, and other Ukrainians think they're sycophantic Putler-loving assholes. Which they basically are.

Separatist
Сепаратист
This is most basic, straightforward term for Ukrainians who long for a return to the Russian fold. Most of them live in the eastern part of the country known as the Donbass region. That's where most of the fighting is.

Colorados
Колорады
This comes from the black and orange Saint George ribbons that the separatist fighters wear, called колорадская лента (*ko-lo-RAD-ska-ya LYEN-ta*/Colorado ribbon).

Down-bass
Даунбасс
As mentioned, most of the separatists live in the Donbass region, sometimes derogatorily referred to as Даунбасс, which combines Донбасс (Donbass) with даун (Down, as in Down's Syndrome). Occasionally also referred to as Донбабве (*don-BAB-ve*), which combines the first part of the toponym Don with the country of Zimbabwe.

Luganda/Lugandon
Луганда/Лугандон
Another major city in Eastern Ukraine is Lugansk. This is also a derogatory term combining Луганск (Lugansk) and the African country Уганда (Uganda).

Gay-ropa
Гейропа
This is an amalgam of gay and Europe, basically mocking the fact that gay rights (and gay marriage) are actually a thing in Europe.

Racial slurs
ra-SIST-ski-ye vi-ra-ZHE-ni-ya
Расистские выражения

There ain't nothin' PC about Russian culture, and everything from nasty racial and ethnic slurs to the ubiquitous *Chukchi* jokes are fairly common. Chukchi are an indigenous people of the Russian far east, and if you've never heard a *Chukcha* joke, they're usually something along these lines:

Why does the Chukcha open yogurt in the store? Because it says "Open here"!
po-che-MU CHUK-cha ot-kri-VA-yet YO-gurt v ma-ga-ZI-nye? po-to-MU chto na nyom na-PI-sa-no: "Ot-KRIT zdyes"!
Почему чукча открывает йогурт в магазине? Потому что на нем написано: "Открыть здесь"!

In other words, like most racist humor, this ain't real clever stuff. Now, I certainly don't advocate using any of the following phrases, but the reality is you'll likely hear them sooner or later, so you may as well be aware of what's what.

Blackass
chyer-no-ZHO-pii
Черножопый
This term describes not only people of African descent, but basically anyone darker skinned than your average Slav, such as Caucasians (i.e., people from the Caucasus region). Here's a little irony for you: In the US, a "Caucasian" is a white person, but to a Russian a "Caucasian" is black. Go figure. You might also hear the term черномазый (*chyerno-MA-zii*) referring to any dark-skinned person. Black people of African origin are usually called негры (*NYE-gri*), which is actually considered a fairly neutral term, unlike its English equivalent.

LKN

el-ka-EN

ЛКН

This stands for лицо кавказкой национальности (*li-TSO kav-KAZ-koi na-sti-o-NAL-nos-ti*), or a person of Caucasian nationality. There is in fact no such thing as a single "Caucasian nationality," and this term can refer to anyone from Armenians, Georgians, and Azeris to Chechens, Ingush, and various ethnic groups of Dagestan.

Caucasian

KHA-chik

ХАчик

Again, meaning someone from the Caucasus region. This term comes from an Armenian name.

Central Asian

u-RYUK

Урюк

You might also hear чурбан (*chur-BAN*) or чурка (*CHUR-ka*).

Ukrainian

kho-KHOL

Хохол

A female Ukrainian is a хохлушка (*kho-KHLUSH-ka*), and Ukraine itself is sometimes referred to as Хохландия (*khokh-LAN-di-ya*).

Belarusian

bul-BASH

Бульбаш

Yank

a-me-ri-KOS

Америкос

You may also hear, юс (*yus*) from "US", and, of course Янки (*YANki*). There is also the word пиндос (*pin-DOS*), which used to apply to American military serving abroad, but is now often used for Americans in general. From this comes the slang term for America, Пиндосия (*pin-DO-si-ya*).

Yid
zhid
Жид
Israel is also sometimes referred to as Жидовия (*zhi-DO-vi-ya*). You may also here the words зяма (*ZYA-ma*) and Рабинович (*ra-biNO-vich*) in reference to Jews.

Slit eye
uz-ko-GLA-zii
Узкоглазый

Russky
mos-KAL
Москаль
This term is mainly used by Ukrainians to refer to their sometimes not-so-friendly neighbors. You might also hear русак (*ru-SAK*) and кацап (*ka-TSAP*).

Shit talkin'
go-vo-RIT der-MO
Говорить Дерьмо

I don't know what it is about talking shit about other people, but it just feels good. From ridiculing friends and family members to railing on total strangers, it's good, clean fun to grossly exaggerate—if not outright fabricate—various personal weaknesses for your own entertainment.

He's a shit-talker.
on piz-DUN.
Он пиздун.

He's a liar.
on vrun.
Он врун.

He always talks nonsense.
on po-sto-YA-nno bryed nye-SYOT.
Он постоянно бред несёт.

He thinks he's all that.
on schi-TA-yet se-BYA kru-TIM.
Он считает себя крутым.

What, can't you see he's just a **screwball?**
ti CHTO, nye VI-dish, chto E-to zhe KLO-un?
Ты что, не видишь, что это же **клоун**?

She's lost her fucking mind.
o-NA piz-da-NU-las.
Она пизданулась.

He does everything **half assed.**
on vsyo DYEL-a-yet v pyen ko-LO-du.
Он всё делает **в пень колоду**.

He's the **biggest dickhead** I have ever seen.
ta-KO-vo VSHI-vo-vo piz-DYU-ka ya ye-SCHO nye vi-DAL.
Такого **вшивого пиздюка** я ещё не видал.

Just look at that **loser**—what a freak!
ti po-smo-TRI na E-to-vo LU-ze-ra—ta-KOI u-ROD!
Ты посмотри на этого **лузера**—такой урод!

He's a fucking zero.
on vo-ob-SCHE piz-do-YOB.
Он вообще пиздоёб.

He's such a **douche bag** and I'm sick of all his **frontin'.**
on ta-KOI gon-DON i mnye na-do-YE-li ye-VO pon-TI.
Он такой **гондон** и мне надоели его **понты**.

She's such an **idiot.**
o-NA ta-KA-ya DU-ra.
Она такая **дура**.

NAME-CALLING
OB-ZI-VA-NI-YE
ОБЗЫВАНИЕ

Bitch!
SU-ka!
Сука!
(used for both
males and
females)

Son of a bitch!
SU-kin sin!
Сукин сын!

Bastard!
PAD-la!
Падла!

Dummy!
ba-RAN!
Баран!

Wacko!
byez-BA-she-nnii!
Безбашенный!

Asshole!
mu-DAK!
Мудак!

Dumbass!
mu-DI-lo!
Мудило!

Shithead!
dol-bo-YOB!
Долбоёб!

Little shit!
piz-DYUK!
Пиздюк!

Jackass!
ko-ZYOL!
Козёл!

Freak!
u-ROD!
Урод!

Prick!
pod-LYETS!
Подлец!

Retard!
dye-fyek-TIV-nii!
Дефективный!

Dirty ass prick!
khui nye-MI-tii
Хуй немытый!

Scumbag!
po-DO-nok!
Подонок!

Dipshit!
lokh!
Лох!

Moron!
de-BIL!
Дебил!

Psycho!
psikh!
Псих!

Cocksucker!
khu-ye-SOS!
Хуесос!

Fucking whore!
BLYAD-ska-ya piz-do-YO-bi-na!
Блядская пиздоёбина!

Fuckbrain!
moz-go-YOB!
Мозгоёб!

Fucking bitch!
SU-ka zlo-ye-BU-cha-ya!
Сука злоебучая!

Fucking piece of shit!
YO-ba-nnii za-SRA-nyets!
Ёбанный засранец!

She's such a **wench**.
o-NA ta-KA-ya STYER-va.
Она такая **стерва**.

I'm sick of her **bitchiness**.
mnye na-do-YE-la ye-YO VRYED-nost.
Мне надоела её **вредность**.

He thinks he's **hot shit**.
on chi-TA-yet se-BYA khu-YOM VAZH-nim.
Он считает себя **хуём важным**.

He's kind of a **weirdo**.
u nye-VO ta-ra-KA-ni v go-lo-VYE.
У него **тараканы в голове**.
Literally, "he's got cockroaches in his head."

He throws all his dough away on trash.
on vi-BRA-si-va-yet svo-YO ba-BLO na ba-ra-KHLO.
Он выбрасывает своё бабло на барахло.

He always takes the bus because he's such a **tightwad**.
on vseg-DA YEZ-dit na av-TO-bu-sye po-to-MU chto yeVO ZHA-ba DU-shit.
Он всегда ездит на автобусе, потому что его **жаба душит**.
The image conveyed by this term is literally of someone being strangled by a toad.

I'm irked by ....
me-NYA BYE-sit (singular)....*me-NYA BYE-syat* (plural)....
Меня бесит.…/Меня бесят.…

> **your idiotic grin**
> *tvo-YA i-di-OT-ska-ya u-LIB-ka*
> твоя идиотская улыбка

> **your stanky armpits**
> *tvo-I vo-NYU-chi-ye pod-MIH-ki*
> твои вонючие подмышки

your slutty girlfriend
tvo-YA BLYAD-ska-ya po-DRUZH-ka
твоя блядская подружка

your stupid ideas
tvo-I du-RAT-ski-ye i-dye-I
твои дурацкие идеи

your endless jabber
tvo-YA byes-ko-NYECH-na-ya bol-tov-NYA
твоя бесконечная болтовня

Talkin' shit
ob-si-RA-ni-ye
Обсирание

Don't be a smart aleck!
nye UM-ni-chai!
Не умничай!

Stop being such a wanker!
KHVA-tit kha-MIT!
Хватит хамить!

Don't ask me such stupid questions!
nye za-da-VAI mnye du-RATS-ki-kh vo-PRO-sov!
Не задавай мне дурацких вопросов!

Shut your piehole!
past za-KHLOP-ni!
Пасть захлопни!

You fucking moron!
dol-bo-YOB!
Долбоёб!

Shut your fucking mouth already!
zat-KNI ye-BA-lo u-ZHE!
Заткни ебало уже!

Drop dead!
chtob ti SDOKH!
Чтоб ты сдох!

Eat shit and die!
zhri gov-NO i SDOKH-ni!
Жри говно и сдохни!

Shove it up your ass!
khui te-BYE v ZHO-pu!
Хуй тебе в жопу!

You stinking bastard!
u-BLYU-dok vo-NYU-chii!
Ублюдок вонючий!

Kickin' ass
mor-do-BOI
Мордобой

When it's time to really get your game on and make your ass-kicking intentions known, these phrases won't leave 'em guessing about how the night is gonna end. So get out your brass knuckles, update your insurance policy, and let's rumble, Russian style!

What, you cruisin' for a bruisin'?
ti CHTO, KHO-chesh MA-khach?
Ты что, хочешь махач?

You think you can kick my ass?
ti DU-ma-yesh, shto MO-zhesh mye-NYA ot-mu-DO-khat?
Ты думаешь, что меня можешь меня отмудохать?

You want a piece of this?
ti CHO, KHO-chesh piz-DI po-lu-CHIT?
Ты чё, хочешь пизды получить?

On your knees, bitch!
na ko-LYE-ni, SU-ka!
На колени, сука!

If you come near me again...
YES-li ye-SCHO raz ko MNYE po-do-i-DYOSH...
Если ещё раз ко мне подойдёшь…

If you don't shut your mouth...
YES-li nye za-KRO-yesh rot...
Если не закроешь рот…

> **I'm gonna beat the shit out of you!**
> *ya te-BYA ot-PI-zhu!*
> я тебя отпизжу!

> **I'm gonna open a can of whoop ass on you!**
> *ya te-BYA pye-rre-khu-YA-ryu!*
> я тебя перехуярю!

> **I'm gonna kick your ass!**
> *ya te-BYA vye-BYU!*
> я тебя въебу!

> **I'm gonna fuck you up!**
> *ya tye-BYE dam piz-DI!*
> я тебе дам пизды!

> **I'll kick you in the nuts!**
> *ya tye-BYE dam po YAI-tsam!*
> я тебе дам по яйцам!

I'll crack your nuts wide open!
ya te-BYE SDYE-la-yu YICH-ni-tsu!
я тебе сделаю яичницу!
Literally, "I'll make you scrambled eggs." If you recall, in Russian, balls are called "eggs."

I'm going to kill you!
ya te-BYA GROKH-nu!
я тебя грохну!

I'm gonna ice you!
ya te-BYA za-mo-CHU!
я тебя замочу!

I'm going to rearrange your face!
ya te-BYE na-CHI-schu RI-lo!
я тебе начищу рыло!

I'm going to bash your fuckin' face in!
ya te-BYE VRYE-zhu po ye-BA-lu!
я тебе врежу по ебалу!

I'm gonna own you, bitch!
ya te-BYA VI-ye-blyu, SU-ka!
я тебя выеблю, сука!

....

Relax!
ras-SLAB-sya!
Расслабься!

Use these if you wuss out at the last minute...

Calm down!
us-po-KOI-sya!
Успокойся!

Get a grip!
voz-MI se-BYA v RU-ki!
Возьми себя в руки!

Come to your senses!
o-POM-nis!
Опомнись!

Everything's under control here.
VSYO tut pod kon-TROL-yem.
Всё тут под контролем.

No questions/I got it.
ba-ZA-rov nyet.
Базаров нет.

Whatever you say.
kak SKA-zhesh.
Как скажешь.

Let's forget about it.
pro-YE-kha-li.
Проехали.

Shit happens.
piz-DA ru-LYU.
Пизда рулю.

Indifference
rav-no-DU-shi-ye
Равнодушие

They say the opposite of love isn't hate; it's indifference.
So if you really wanna piss someone off, just tell them how
little you care.

I don't give a care.
mnye PO fi-gu.
Мне по фигу.

I couldn't care less.
mnye po ba-ra-BA-nu.
Мне по барабану.

I don't give a shit.
mnye na-SRAT.
Мне насрать.

I don't give a damn.
mnye na-plye-VAT.
Мне наплевать.

Makes no difference to me.
da mnye ab-so-LYUT-no fi-o-LYE-to-vo.
Да мне абсолютно фиолетово.

I don't give a fuck.
me-NYA E-to nye ye-BYOT.
Меня это не ебёт.

What the hell do I need your problems for?
na fi-GA mnye nuzh-NI tvo-I pro-BLYE-mi?
На фига мне нужны твои проблемы?

Ah, fuck it.
nu, KHUI s nim.
Ну, хуй с ним.

What the fuck do I need this for?
na-khu-YA mnye E-to NA-do?
Нахуя мне это надо?

This is fucking boring.
mnye E-to os-to-ye-BLO.
Мне это остоебло.

What the hell do I care?
nu, a mnye ka-KOI khryen?
Ну, а мне какой хрен?

And what do I have to do with it?
a ya tut pri-CHOM?
А я тут причём?

That's all I need!
TOL-ko E-to-vo mnye nye khva-TA-yet!
Только этого мне не хватает!

To fuck with it all!
ye-BIS vsyo ko-NYOM!
Ебись всё конём!

....

Disbelief
nye-do-VYER-i-ye
Недоверие

Most people are full of crap. I say, call them out and tell them straight up that you ain't buyin' what they're sellin'.

You gotta be kidding me!
da ti chto!
Да ты что!

What a load of crap!
chto za che-pu-KHA!
Что за чепуха!

That's doggy doo!
E-to chuzh so-BA-chya!
Это чушь собачья!

That's dumb!
E-to ga-LI-mo!
Это галимо!

That's nonsense!
E-to NON-sens!
Это нонсенс!

Cut the bullshit.
KHVA-tit piz-DYET.
Хватит пиздеть.

Don't try to play me.
nye NA-do mnye lap-SHU na U-shi VYE-shat.
Не надо мне лапшу на уши вешать.
Literally, "don't hang noodles from my ears." Now just try to tell me that
Russian isn't the coolest language ever.

That's a total joke!
vot E-to pri-KOL!
Вот это прикол!

Well, that's a surprise!
vot E-to po-vo-ROT!
Вот это поворот!

That's nuts!
s u-MA so-i-TI!
С ума сойти!

This is a madhouse!
E-to dur-DOM!
Это дурдом!

CHAPTER 7

Music & Technology
MU-zy-ka i tekh-no-LO-gi-ya
Музыка и Технология

There's no denying it: Russian pop music sucks. Fortunately, there are a number of decent alternative and hard-core bands to make up for it. In terms of language, you'll probably be happy to know that the vast majority of words related to music and pop culture in Russia are just English words pronounced with a Russified accent. So really, the more English you speak when discussing topics of pop culture, the hipper you'll sound.

Musical genres
mu-zi-KALni-ye ZHAN-ri
Музыкальные жанры

Let's listen to some....
Da-VAI po-SLUsha-yem....
Давай послушаем ...

God I hate....
tyer-PYET nye mo-GU ...
Терпеть не могу....

Rock 'n' roll
rok-n-roll
Рок-н-ролл

Pop
pop-SA
Попса

Alternative
al-tyer-na-TI-va
Альтернатива

Heavy metal
KHE-vi-ME-tal
Хэви-метал

Punk rock
pank-rok
Панк-рок

Ska
ska
Ска

Reggae
RE-ggei/RE-ggi
Реггей/Регги

Rap/Hip-hop
rep/khip-KHOP
Рэп/Хип-хоп

Indie
IN-di-rok
Инди-рок

Funk
fank
Фанк

Jazz

jaz

Джаз

"Author music"

AV-tor-ska-ya MU-zi-ka

Авторская музыка

This refers to the so-called барды (*BAR-di*) of the Russian musical tradition. It sometimes sounds like folk rock, is often acoustic, and the main criterion is that the singer write his own lyrics. Two of the most famous examples are Владимир Высоцкий (Vladimir Vysotsky) and Булат Окуджава (Bulat Okudzhava). Both are dead but still listened to a lot more often than many living singers.

Shanson

shan-SON

Шансон

If you take cabs in Russia, likely you'll become well acquainted with Shanson. This was originally the music of criminals and wannabe thugs, but now it's all over the place. A good example of this genre is the late Михаил Круг (Mikhail Krug) and his strangely catchy ballad Владимирский централ (Vladimirskii Tsentral). This music is also sometimes referred to as Блатная музыка (*blat-NA-ya MU-zi-ka*), a term that betrays its prison camp origins.

Industrial

in-dus-tri-AL-na-ya

Индустриальная

R&B

air-en-bi

Айренби

Country

KAN-tri

Кантри

Blues

blyuz

Блюз

CHASTUSHKI
CHAS-TUSH-KI
ЧАСТУШКИ

Chastushki are sort of like Russian limericks set to music, usually accompanied by an accordion, and sung off key either by a drunken, sweaty *muzhik* or a *baba* with a whiny voice trying to sound folksy. But on the upside, they're usually pretty funny, at least if you've had a few drinks. Here are a couple examples. Note that these translations are more artistic than literal.

Я с милёнком целовалась,
Целовалась горячо.
Я ещё бы целовалась,
Да болит влагалищо.

ya s mi-LYON-kom tse-lo-VA-las,
tse-lo-VA-las go-rya-CHO.
ya ye-SCHO bi tse-lo-VA-las,
da bo-LIT vla-GA-li-scho.

Me and my honey did some kissing,
We are hot and heavy flirts.
I would like to kiss him more,
But my vagina already hurts.

Отведу мою милашку
к зелёному дубу.
Пусть её ебёт медведь,
Я больше не буду.

ot-vye-DU mo-YU mi-LASH-ku
k zye-LYO-no-mu DU-bu.
pust ye-YO ye-BYOT myed-VYED,
ya BOL-she nye BU-du.

I'm gonna take my girl
Away to the green oak woods.
Let some bear fuck her there,
I've had enough of her goods.

Disco
DIS-ko
Диско

Acoustic
a-KUS-ti-ka
Акустика

Electronic music
e-lyek-TRO-na-ya MU-zi-ka
Электронная музыка

Russian stage music
ro-SSII-ska-ya es-TRA-da
Российская эстрада

Middle-aged Russians love this stuff, and you'll be lucky if you can escape a trip to Russia without being subjected to the musical stylings of pop diva Алла Борисовна Пугачёва (Alla Borisovna Pugacheva), Russia's answer to Barbra Streisand, and her former husband, the freakishly flamboyant Филипп Киркоров (Filipp Kirkorov). On the other hand, the more hard-rockin' act Любэ (Lyube) isn't half bad if you're into civilians dressing up in military uniform and singing the praises of the armed forces.

In the band
v BEN-dye
В бэнде

That's really a cool **band**!
E-to KLASS_nii bend!
Это классный **бэнд**!

They're an awesome **group**!
o-NI o-bal-DYE-nna-ya GRU-ppa!
Они обалденная **группа**!

I really like Leningrad's new **album**.
mnye O-chen NRA-vi-tsya NO-vii al-BOM lye-nin-GRA-da.
Мне очень нравится новый **альбом** Ленинграда.

I hear DDT is going **on tour** this summer.
ya SLI-shal, chto DDT LYE-tom YE-dut na ga-STRO-li.
Я слышал, что ДДТ летом приедут на **гастроли**.

Zemfira's new song is a real **hit**.
*NO-va-ya PYES-nya zem-FI-ri—na-sto-YA-schii **khit***.
Новая песня Земфиры—настоящий **хит**.

That song is just too **poppy**.
E-ta PYES-nya SLISH-kom pop-SO-va-ya.
Эта песня слишком **попсовая**.

I dig the **rhythm** of reggae.
*ya ta-SCHUS ot **RIT-ma** RE-ggi*.
Я тащусь от **ритма** регги.

I went to an amazing **concert** last night.
*ya vchye-RA kho-DIL na o-fi-GYE-nnii **kon-TSERT***.
Я вчера ходил на офигенный **концерт**.

My friend works as a **DJ** at radio station.
*moi drug ra-BO-ta-yet **di-je-yem** na ra-di-o-
STAN-tsii*.
Мой друг работает ди-**джеем** на
радиостанции.

Is all music in **Russia really pirated**?
*nye-u-ZHE-li vsya MU-zy-ka v ro-SSII **pi-RAT-ska-ya***?
Неужели вся музыка в России **пиратская**?

Is **twerking** popular in Russia?
TVER-king *po-pu-LYAR-nii v ro-SII*?
Тверкинг - популярный в России?

I'm a big **fan** of Pussy Riot.
*ya bol-ZHOI **po-KLO-nnik** pussy riot*.
Я большой **поклонник** Pussy Riot.

That **pop** star always gives autographs to his **fans**.
*E-ta **pop-zvyez-DA** vsyeg-DA da-YOT svo-IM **fa-NATkam**
av-TO-gra-fi*.
Эта **поп-звезда** всегда даёт своим **фанаткам** автографы.

I'm a total **music freak!**
ya vo-ob-SCHE mye-lo-MAN!
Я вообще **меломан!**

Backing track
mi-nu-SOV-ka
Минусовка
These are used for singers to essentially perform karaoke-style on stage.

Recorded song
fa-NYE-ra
Фанера
Pop stars lip-synch along with Фанера on stage.

Guitar amp
pri-MOCH-ka
Примочка

Rehearsal
RYE-pa
Репа
This is short for репетиция (*rye-pye-TI-tsi-ya*).

PC speak
PC sleng
РС сленг

There's a good reason that every Russian living in the US.seems to work as a computer programmer. Russians kick ass at this shit, and they are known to be some of the most skilled hackers around. You know that last virus your computer caught? Likely it was created by some Russian teenager just goofing around after class. So why can't they come up with their own words for PC speak?

My **operating system** fucking crashed again.
mo-YA o-pye-ra-TSON-ka o-PYAT piz-DOI na-KRI-las.
Моя **операционка** опять пиздой накрылась.

My computer is infected with a **virus**.
moi kom-PYU-ter zaRA-zhen VI-ru-som.
Мой компьютер заражен **вирусом**.

I don't know how to **use** a Mac.
ya nye u-MYE-yu YU-zat mak.
Я не умею **юзать** Мак.
From the English verb "to use."

I'll **scan** it for you.
ya te-BYE ot-ska-NI-ru-yu.
Я тебе **отсканирую**.
From the English verb "to scan."

For some reason, I can't **attach** this **file**.
CHTO-to nye mo-GU pri-a-TTA-chit E-tot fail.
Что-то не могу **приаттачить** этот **файл**.
Both from English words: "attach" and "file."

If you **download** the program, I can install it for you.
*YES-li ska-CHA-yesh E-tu pro-GRA-mmu, ya po-mo-GU te-BYE
u-sta-no-VIT.*
Если **скачаешь** эту программу, я помогу тебе установить.

He has always tried to keep up with **technology**.
on VSYEG-da sta-RAL-sya id-TI v NO-gu s tyekh-no-LO-giye.
Он всегда старался идти в ногу с **технологией**.

Start-ups in Silicon Valley are always on the lookout for angel
investors.
start-API *v krem-ni-YE-voi do-LI-nye po-sto-YA-nno v POI-skakh
BIZ-nyes AN-gye-lov.*
Стартапы в Кремниевой долине постоянно в поисках бизнес-
ангелов.

Hackathon
KHA-a-ton
Хакатон
Hacker (Хакер/*KHA-ker*) and hacking (Хакинг/*KHA-king*) have become such popular terms that лайфхак (lifehack) has also entered the language.

Cell (phone)
mo-BIL-ka
Мобилка
Also sometimes мобила (*mo-BI-la*) or сотовый (*SO-to-vii*).

To text
tyek-sto-VAT
Текстовать

SMS
es-em-ES-ka
СМС-ка
Sometimes spelled out phonetically as эсэмэска.

I downloaded a new **mobile app** for my smartphone.
*ya ska-CHAL NO-vo-ye **mo-BIL-no-ye pri-lo-ZHE-ni-ye** dlya mo-YE-vo smart-fo-na.*
Я скачал новое **мобильное приложение** для моего смартфона.

The touchscreen on my **tablet** is cracked.
*touch-SCREEN na mo-YOM **plan-SHE-tye** TRYES-nul.*
Тачскрин на моём **планшете** треснул.

I need to fix the **touchscreen** on my Android.
*mne NA-do po-chi-NIT **SYEN-sor-nii E-kran** na mo-YOM an-DROI-dye.*
Мне надо починить **сенсорный экран** на моём андроиде.

I almost died to get this **selfie**!

ya chut ne po-GIB-la, CHTO-bi SDYE-lat E-to SEL-fi!

Я чуть не погибла, чтобы сделать это **селфи**!

Send me a **screenshot**.

skin mnye skrin-SHOT.

Скинь мне **скриншот**.

Do they have **wi-fi** here?

Tut YEST vai-FAI?

Тут есть **Вай-Фай**?

The World Wide Web

myezh-du-na-ROD-na-ya syet

Международная сеть

While the World Wide Web is indeed worldwide, Russia has carved out its own little corner referred to as Рунет (*Runet*).

I really liked her **profile**.

mnye O-chen po-NYA-vil-sya ye-YO PRO-fil.

Мне очень понравился её **профиль**.

We got to know each better in a **chat room**.

mi po-zna-KO-mi-lis po-BLI-zhe SI-dya v CHA-tye.

Мы познакомились поближе сидя в **чате**.

She sent me a **PM**.

o-NA na-pi-SA-la mnye v LICH-ku.

Она написала мне в **личку**.

We still haven't met **IRL**.

mi ye-SCHO nye VSTRYE-ti-lis v re-A-lye.

Мы ещё не встретились **в реале**.

She has sent me some pics **by e-mail**.

o-NA mnye FOT-ki SKI-nula po MI-lu.

Она мне фотки скинула **по мылу**.

If **anyone** doubts our love, they should see all the **emoticons** we use.

*YES-li **kto-nit** som-nye-VA-ye-tsya v NA-shei lyub-VI, o-NI bi u-VI-dye-li ka-KI-ye mi is-POL-zu-yem **SMAI-li-ki**.*

Если **кто-нить** сомневается в нашей любви, они бы увидели какие мы используем **смайлики**.

You can read all about it on my **blog**.

*MOZH-no o-bo VSYOM pro-chi-TAT na mo-YOM **BLO-gye**.*

Можно обо всём прочитать на моём **блоге**.

And not surprisingly, a blogger is called a блоггер (*BLOG-ger*).

Internet trolls always ruin my favorite forums.

in-ter-NET TROL-li *vsyeg-DA POR-tyat mo-I lyu-BI-mi-ye FO-ru-mi.*

Интернет тролли всегда портят мои любимые форумы.

I am so sick of **spam**.

mnye tak na-do-YEL spam.

Мне так надоел **спам**.

I spend a lot of time on the **web**.

*ya MNO-go VRYE-mye-ni pro-vo-ZHU v **sye-TI**.*

Я много времени провожу в **сети**.

I flamed some idiot and got **banned**.

*ya SDYE-lal ka-KO-mu-to i-di-O-tu **fleim** i po-lu-CHIL **ban**.*

Я сделал какому-то идиоту **флейм** и получил **бан**.

For some reason I can't **download** Skype on my iPad.

*ya po-chye-MU-to nye mo-GU **ska-CHAT** skaip na moi ai-PAD.*

Я почему-то не могу **скачать** Скайп на мой айпад.

I'll send you the link to my **web page**.

*ya te-BYE po-SHLU SSIL-ku na mo-YU **veb-stra-NI-tsu**.*

Я тебе пошлю ссылку на мою **веб-страницу**.

Do you have an **e-mail address**?

*u te-BYA YEST **A-dryes e-lyek-TRO-nnoi POCH-ti**?*

У тебя есть **адрес электронной почты**?

My e-mail is...
moi e-meil...
Мой е-мэйл…
The symbol @ used in e-mail addresses is pronounced as собачка (*so-BACH-ka*). You may also hear e-mail called мыло (*MI-lo*), which literally means soap, but I guess kinda sounds like the English word mail.

Now the fucking **site** won't accept my **log-in and password.**
*tye-PYER E-tot YO-ba-nnii **sait** nye pri-ni-MA-yet mo-YO **I-mya POL-zo-va-tye-lya** i pa-ROL.*
Теперь этот ёбанный **сайт** не принимает моё **имя пользователя и пароль.**

I often listen to **podcasts** about the upcoming Zombie apocalypse.
*ya CHAS-to SLU-sha-yu **AU-di-o pod-KAS-ti** o pryed-sto-YA-shem ZOM-bi apo-ka-LIP-si-sye.*
Я часто слушаю **аудио подкасты** о предстоящем зомби-апокалипсисе.

Where can I find a **livestream** of the game?
*Gdye MOZH-no na-i-ti **LIVE-stream** MAT-cha?*
Где можно найти **лайвстрим** матча?

Social media
sots-se-TI
Соцсети

What **social media** do you use?
*ka-KI-mi **so-TSIAL-ni-mi sye-TYAMI** ti POL-zu-yesh-sya?*
Какими **социальными сетями** ты пользуешься?

I have a page on VKontakte.
u me-NYA yest svo-YA stra-NI-tsa v Vkon-TAK-tye.
У меня есть своя страница в ВКонтакте.
This is probably the most popular Runet social media site.

I just **registered** on odnoklassniki.ru.

ya TOL-ko chto za-rye-gi-STRI-ro-val-sya na od-noKLASS-ni-kakh TOCH-ka ru.

Я только что **зарегистрировался** на одноклассники.ru.

This is also a pretty popular social networking site, but it seems to be losing out to VKontakte lately.

My username is...

moi nik...

Мой ник...

My feed is always full of spam.

v svo-YE LYEN-tye po-sto-YAN-no KU-cha SPAM-a.

В своей ленте постоянно куча спама.

What's trending now?

chto SEI-chas v TRYEN-dye?

Что сейчас в тренде?

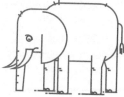

In my free time, I like to troll Republicans on social media.

v svo-BOD-no-ye VRE-mya, ya LYU-BLYU TROL-lit res-pub-li-KAN-tsev v so-TSIAL-nikh SYE-takh.

В свободное время, я люблю троллить Республиканцев в социальных сетях.

I'm starting to clean out my friends list on Facebook.

na-chi-NA-yu za-CHIST-ku FREN-dov na FACE-book-ye.

Начинаю зачистку френдов на Фейсбуке.

His meme started a new Instagram trend.

ye-VO mem NA-chal NO-vii TRENDinsta-GRAM-a.

Его мем начал новый тренд Инстаграма.

I found this video trending on YouTube.

ya na-SHOL E-to VI-de-o v TREN-dye na you-TU-bye.

Я нашёл это видео в тренде на Ютубе.

The meme with Putin without his shirt instantly **went viral**.
*mem PU-ti-na byez ru-BASH-ki mgno-VYEN-no **stal
me-di-a-VI-ru-som**.*
Мем Путина без рубашки мгновенно **стал медиавирусом**.

I "liked" your new post.
*ya po-STA-vil **like** na tvoi NO-vii post.*
Я поставил **лайк** на твой новый пост.

The pic of a cloud that looks like Jesus Christ instantly became
a **viral meme**.
*FOT-ka O-bla-ka, ko-TO-ro-ye po-KHO-zha na i-SU-sa khris-TA BY-
stro **STA-la VI-rus-nim ME-mom**.*
Фотка облака, которое похоже на Исуса Христа быстро **стала
вирусным мемом**.

Can you **repost** my tweet?
*ty MO-zhesh **re-POS-tit** moi tvit?*
Ты можешь **репостить** мой твит?

How many **followers** do you have on Twitter?
*SKOL-ko u tye-BYA **FOL-lo-vyer-ov** na TVIT-ter-ye?*
Сколько у тебя **фолловеров** на Твиттере?

What the heck is a **hashtag**?
*CHTO-ta-KO-ye **khesh-TEG**?*
Что такое **хэштег**?

Which **tags** are the most popular?
*ka-KI-ye **TE-gi** na-i-BO-lye-ye po-pu-LYAR-ni?*
Какие **теги** наиболее популярны?

Are you on Snapchat?
ty POL-zu-yesh-sya snap-CHAT-ом?
Ты пользуешься Снапчатом?

I don't have time for **media activism**.
*u mye-NYA nyet VRE-me-ni dlya **ME-di-a ak-ti-VIZ-ma**.*
У меня нет времени для **медиа активизма**.

LOL
r-ZHA-ka
Ржака

The denizens of Runet make frequent use of abbreviations
and acronyms, just like English Internet language.

ИМХО
This is a direct transliteration from the English "IMHO." Also, you'll also
sometimes see ПМСМ (по моему скромному мнению po/*MO-ye-mu
SKROM-no-my MNE-ni-yu*), or even just the English acronym IMHO.

PPKS
ППКС
Stands for подпишусь под каждым словом (*pod-pi-SHUS pod KAZH-dim
SLO-vom*), the equivalent of the English ITA (I Totally Agree).

ЗЫ
If you turn on the Russian keyboard and hit the keys that correspond to
the Latin letters PS, this is what you get. Hence, it means "PS."

IYKWIM
ЕВПОЧЯ
Stands for если вы понимаете о чем я ("if you understand what I'm
talking about").

BRB
брб
Sometimes, the English acronym is so entrenched that there's no sense
in trying to come up with something new.

IDK
ХЗ
This stands for хуй знает, which is more who the fuck knows.

You crack me up.
rzhu-ni-ma-GU
Ржунимагу
From ржу–не могу.

CHAPTER 8

Sports & Games
SPORT i I-gry
Спорт и Игры

Ah, sports. The Soviet Union was legendary for them and for all the gold medals Soviet athletes won in the Olympics. Although those glory days may be fading into the past, sports are still a pretty big deal in Russia, especially soccer and hockey, even though the best of the players have fled abroad for greater fame, more lucrative endorsements, and far better training facilities. Sports in Russia are reputed to be very closely connected to organized crime. That's no surprise, really: Where there is money to be made, there are always people looking for their cut.

I'm into sports

ya u-vlye-KA-yus SPOR-tom
Я увлекаюсь спортом

Who do you **root** for—Dinamo or Spartak?
za ko-VO ti bo-LYE-yesh—za di-NA-mo ili spar-TAK?
За кого ты **болеешь**—за Динамо или Спартак?

I'm rooting for Russia.
ya bo-LYE-yu za ro-SSI-yu.
Я болею за Россию.

Who's the favorite?
kto fa-vo-RIT?
Кто фаворит?

I always pull for the underdog.
*ya vsyeg-DA bo-LYE-yu za **an-dyer-DOG**.*
Я всегда болею за **андердог**.

Let's grab a beer at halftime.
*da-VAI za PI-vom vo VRYE-mya **PA-uzi**.*
Давай за пивом во время **паузы**.

What half is it now?
*ka-KOI sei-CHAS **taim**?*
Какой сейчас **тайм**?

The opposing team sucks balls.
so-PYER-ni-ki—pi-de-RA-si!
Соперники—пидарасы!

We got beat in overtime.
*nas ob-i-GRA-li v **do-pol-NI-tyel-no-ye VRYE-mya**.*
Нас обыграли в **дополнительное время**.

Real fans don't like glory hunters.
*na-sto-YA-shi-ye **bo-LYEL-schi-ki** nye LYU-byat **kuzmi-CHO-va**.*
Настоящие **болельщики** не любят **Кузьмичёва**.

Do you think he dopes?
*kak ti DU-ma-yesh, on pri-ni-MA-yet **DO-ping**?*
Как ты думаешь, он **принимает допинг**?

He's open!
on ot-KRIT!
Он открыт!

The Olympic Games
o-lim-PIIS-ki-ye I-gri
Олимпийские игры

What are Russia's chances at the **Olympics** this year?
*ka-KI-ye u ro-SSII SHAN-si na **o-lim-pi-A-dye** v E-tom go-DU?*
Какие у России шансы на **Олимпиаде** в этом году?

Do you think Russia will win any **gold medals?**
*kak ti DU-ma-yesh, vi-i-GRA-yet li ro-SSI-ya **zo-lo-TI-ye mye-DA-li**?*
Как ты думаешь, выиграет ли Россия **золотые медали**?

Honored Master of Sports
za-SLU-zhe-nii MAS-ter SPOR-ta ro-SSII
Заслуженный мастер спорта России
This is the title given to Russia's most accomplished athletes, similar to a Hall of Famer.

The major sports
GLAV-ni-ye VI-di SPOR-ta
Главные виды спорта

Hockey
kho-KKYEI
Хоккей

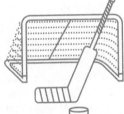

Stanley Cup
KU-bok STYE-nli
Кубок Стэнли
There's also the Hockey World Championship, or Чемпионат мира по хоккею (*chem-pi-o-NAT MI-ra po kho-KYE-yu*).

Did you see how he slammed that **puck** in the net?
*ti VI-dyel, kak on za-BRO-sil **SHAI-bu** v SYET-ku?*
Ты видел, как он забросил **шайбу** в сетку?

Hey, he should get a **penalty shot** for that!
ei, on DOL-zhen za E-to po-lu-CHIT BU-llit!
Эй, он должен за это получить **буллит**!

What's the penalty for **boarding**?
ka-KOI shtraf na tol-CHOK na bort?
Какой штраф на **толчок на борт**?

Soccer
fut-BOL
Футбол
Like most of the world, Russians call soccer "football." If you want to talk
about what Americans call football, it is американский футбол (a-me-ri-
KAN-skii fut-BOL), or American football.

Goalie
vra-TAR
Вратарь

Fullback
za-SCHIT-nik
Защитник

Halfback
po-lu-za-SCHIT-nik
Полузащитник

Uh-oh, the ref is pulling out **the yellow card**.
O-pa! KA-zhe-tsya RYE-fe-ri prye-dya-VLYA-yet gorCHICH-nik.
Опа! Кажется рефери предъявляет **горчичник**.

That dipshit just kicked the ball into his own **post**!
E-tot loch TOL-ko chto za-BRO-sil myach v svo-I voRO-ta!
Этот лох только что забросил мяч в свои **ворота**!

Holy shit! He totally scored a **hat trick**!
yob! On vo-ob-SCHE o-FOR-mil khet-trik!
Ёб! Он вообще оформил **хет-трик**!

Goooooooaaaaaaal!
goooooooool!
Гоооооооол!

Please, oh lord, let us win the **penalty shootout**.
GOS-po-di, dai nam VI-i-grat SYE-ri-yu pye-NAL-ti.
Господи, дай нам выиграть **серию пенальти**.

Fuck! Another **draw**!
blyad, o-PYAT ni-CHYA!
Блядь, опять **ничья**!

World Championship of Soccer
chem-pi-o-NAT MI-ra po fut-BOL-u
Чемпионат мира по футболу
Usually abbreviated as ЧМ (*ChM*) or called Кубок мира (*KU-bok MI-ra*, World Cup).

The 4 B's
che-TI-re be
4Б
This stands for the four B's of Russian soccer: Бил, Бью, Буду Бить ("I've scored, I score, I will score"). This was the motto of the famous Russian footballer Aleksandr Kerzhakov.

Who do you think will win the **UEFA** Cup this year?
kak ti DU-ma-yesh, kto vi-i-GRA-yet KU-bok u-ef-a v E-tom go-DU?
Как ты думаешь, кто выиграет **Кубок УЕФА** в этом году?

Tennis
TYE-nnis
Теннис

Anna Kournikova looks smokin' in her **tennis whites**.
A-nna KUR-ni-ko-va o-fi-GYE-nno VI-glya-dit v svo- YOM TYE-nnis-nom ko-STYU-mye.
Анна Курникова офигенно выглядит в своём **теннисном костюме**.

Figure skating
fi-GUR-no-ye ka-TA-ni-ye
Фигурное катание

> The Russian **judges** always cheat.
> *RU-sski-ye **SU-dyi** vsyeg-DA much-LYU-yut.*
> Русские **судьи** всегда мухлюют.

Gymnastics
gim-NAS-ti-ka
Гимнастика

> I bet that **gymnast** would be wild in bed!
> *na-vyer-nya-KA E-ta **gim-NAST-ka** bye-ZUM-na v po-STYE-li!*
> Наверняка эта **гимнастка** безумна в постели!

Boxing
boks
Бокс

Weightlifting
tya-ZHO-la-ya at-LYE-ti-ka
Тяжёлая атлетика

Weightlifter
shtan-GIST
Штангист

> Sure, **steroids** make you strong, but they also make you sterile.
> *ko-NYECH-no **stye-RO-i-d**i DYE-la-yut te-BYA SILnim, no ye-SCHO DYE-la-yut te-BYA byes-PLOD-nim.*
> Конечно **стероиды** делают тебя сильным, но ещё делают тебя бесплодным.

Skiing
ka-TA-ni-ye na LI-zhakh
Катание на лыжах

I hate **cross-country**, but I love **downhill skiing**.
ya nye-na-VI-zhu LIZH-ni-ye GON-ki, no lyu-BLYU GOR-ni-ye LI-zhi.
Я ненавижу **лыжные гонки**, но люблю **горные лыжи**.
Free-style skiing (фристайл) is pronounced like in the English (*fri-STAIL*).

Other kinds of sports
dru-GI-ye VI-di SPOR-ta
Другие виды спорта

Track and field
LYOG-ka-ya at-LYE-ti-ka
Лёгкая атлетика

> That **runner** is a doper.
> *E-tot **bye-GUN**—KHI-mik.*
> Этот **бегун**—химик.

Water sports
VOD-ni-ye VI-di SPOR-ta
Водные виды спорта

Swimming
PLA-va-ni-ye
Плавание
Note that there are two basic verbs meaning "to swim": плавать (*PLA-vat*) refers to something like swimming laps, whereas купаться (*ku-PA-tsya*) is more like going for a dip/goofing around in the water.

Surfing
SYOR-fing
Сёрфинг

Fishing
ri-BAL-ka
Рыбалка

Extreme sports
ek-STRIM sport
Экстрим спорт

Skateboarding
skeit-BOR-ding
Скейтбординг
Sometimes just called скейт (*skeit*).

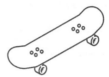

Snowboarding
sno-u-BOR-ding
Сноубординг

Skydiving
prizh-kI s pa-ra-SHU-tom
Прыжки с парашютом

Rock climbing
ska-lo-LA-za-ni-ye
Скалолазание

Auto racing
av-to-GON-ki
Автогонки

Drag racing
drag REI-sing
Драг рейсинг

MARTIAL ARTS
BO-YE-VI-YE IS-KU-SSTVA
БОЕВЫЕИСКУССТВА

Judo	*jyu-DO*	Дзюдо
Karate	*ka-ra-TE*	каратэ
Aikido	*ai-ki-DO*	айкидо
Jujitsu	*ji-u-JIT-su*	Джиу-джитсу
Taekwondo	*tae-kvon-DO*	таэквон-до

Exercise

u-prazh-NYE-ni-ye

Упражнение

I do...

ya za-ni-MA-yus...

Я занимаюсь…

Remember, this verb takes the instrumental case.

> **yoga**
> *YO-goi*
> йогой
>
> **aerobics**
> *ae-RO-bi-koi*
> аэробикой
>
> **bodybuilding**
> *bo-di-BIL-din-gom*
> бодибилдингом
>
> **powerlifting**
> *po-uer-LIF-tin-gom*
> пауэрлифтингом
>
> **dance**
> *TAN-tsa-mi*
> танцами

I want to work my ...

ya kho-CHU ka-CHAT ...

Хочу качать …

> **muscles**
> *MISH-tsi*
> мышцы

abs
pryess
пресс

guns (i.e., biceps)
BAN-ki
банки

triceps
TRI-tseps
трицепс

delts
DYEL-tu
дельту

pecs
grud-NI-ye MISH-tsi
грудные мышцы

thighs
BYO-dra
бёдра

calves
I-kri
икры

glutes
ya-go-DI-tsi
ягодицы

Where can I do some pull-ups?
gdye tut MOZH-no DYE-lat pod-TYA-gi-va-ni-ye?
Где тут можно делать подтягивание?

Do you know a good gym?
*ti nye ZNA-yesh kho-RO-shii **trye-ni-RO-voch-nii zal**?*
Ты не знаешь хороший **тренировочный зал**?

DANCING
TAN-TSI
ТАНЦЫ

Ballroom dancing	*BAL-ni-ye TAN-tsi*	Бальные танцы
Ballet	*ba-LYET*	Балет
Folk dancing	*na-ROD-ni-ye TAN-tsi*	Народные танцы
Salsa	*SAL-sa*	Сальса
Belly dancing	*TA-nyets zh i-vo-TA*	танец живота
Tango	*TAN-go*	танго
Hip-hop	*khip KHOP*	Хип-хоп
Swing	*sving*	Свинг

Where can I **work out?**
*gdye MOZH-no **po-trye-ni-ro-VA-tsya**?*
Где можно **потренироваться**?

Do a lot of people **jog** in Russia?
*MNO-gi-ye LYU-di za-ni-MA-yu-tsya **JO-ggin-gom** v ro-SSII?*
Многие люди занимаются **джоггингом** в России?
The answer, by the way, is no.

Game time
po-RA i-GRAT
Пора играть

Let's play some **Frisbee.**
*da-VAI po-i-GRA-yem v **FRIZ-bi**.*
Давай поиграем в **фризби**.
Frisbee is the name of the game, but if you're referring to the actual disk, you'd use the following:

Let's go **bowling.**
*poi-DYOM i-GRAT v **BO-u-ling**.*
Пойдем играть в **боулинг**.

I love games of chance.
ya lyu-BLYU a-ZART-ni-ye I-gri.
Я люблю азартные игры.

I prefer games of skill.
ya pryed-po-chi-TA-yu ko-MMYER-chis-ki-ye I-gri.
Я предпочитаю коммерческие игры.

If you try to **cheat**, I'll blow the whistle on you.
*YES-li po-pi-TA-yesh-sya **mukh-lye-VAT**, ya te-BYA vlo-ZHU.*
Если попытаешься **мухлевать**, я тебя вложу.

Let's play some cards.
da-VAI po-i-GRA-yem v KAR-ti.
Давай поиграем в карты.

Could you teach me to play **chess**?
*ti bi mog me-NYA na-u-CHIT i-GRAT v **SHAKH-ma-ti**?*
Ты бы мог меня научить играть в **шахматы**?

Let's play some....
po-i-GRA-yem v....
Поиграем в....

> **pool**
> *bil-YARD*
> бильярд

> **ping-pong**
> *na-STOL-nii TYE-nnis*
> настольный теннис

> **foosball**
> *KI-kyer*
> кикер

darts

darts

дартс

video games

vi-de-o-I-gri

видеоигры

Do you know how to play...?

ti u-MYE-yesh i-GRAt v...?

Ты умеешь играть в...?

poker

PO-kyer

покер

Durak

du-RAK

дурак

This is without a doubt the most popular card game in Russia. The object of the game is to get rid of all your cards. The last person holding is the *durak*, or fool.

solitaire

pa-SYANS

пасьянс

bridge

Brij

бридж

preference

prye-fe-RANS

Преферанс

This is a popular Russian variation of bridge simplified to be played with fewer cards.

Gambling
GEM-bling
Гэмблинг

But of course, the best thing about sports is the opportunity to make a little easy money off of someone else's hard work.

Illegal gambling
a-ZART-na-ya i-GRA, za-prye-SCHO-nna-ya za-KO-nom
Азартная игра, запрещённая законом

Legal gambling
a-ZART-na-ya i-GRA, raze-rye-SHO-nna-ya za-KO-nom
Азартная игра, разрешённая законом

A bet
STAV-ka
Ставка

Where's the nearest **slots arcade?**
*gdye SA-ma-ya bli-ZHAI-scha-ya **bo-go-DYEL-nya**?*
Где самая ближайщая **богодельня**?

Where can I **place a bet** on the game?
*gdye MOZH-no **za-KLYU-chat pa-RI** na match?*
Где можно **заключать пари** на матч?

What are the odds on the Russian National Team?
ka-KOI kyef na SBOR-nu-yu ro-SSII?
Какой кеф на Сборную России?

Oddsmaker
gan-di-KA-pper
Гандикаппер
Also called a каппер (*KA-pper*) for short.

CHAPTER 9

Food & Coffee
ye-DA i KO-fye
Еда и Кофе

One of the great things about Russia is the food. Russians love homecooking and are generally pretty skilled at preparing it (well, at least the women are). Precooked, prepackaged food called полуфабрикат (*po-lu-fa-bri-KAT*) is widely available, but most Russians won't eat preservative-filled crap. Which brings me to my next point. "Preservative" in Russian is консервант (*kon-ser-VANT*). The Russian cognate презерватив (*prye-zyer-va-TIV*) means condom. When enjoying a meal in Russia, try not to confuse the two.

Let's eat!
da-VAI po-KU-sha-yem!
Давай покушаем!

I'm hungry.
ya GO-lo-dyen/go-lod-NA.
Я голоден/голодна.

Grub
ZHRACH-ka
Жрачка
Another word for this is жратва (*ZHRAT-va*).

I wanna chow down.
kho-CHU po-ZHRAT.
Хочу пожрать.

You'll feel hungry as soon as you start to eat.
a-ppye-TIT pri-KHO-dit vo VRYE-mya ye-DI.
Аппетит приходит во время еды.
This is a common Russian saying.

I'm as hungry as a wolf.
ya GO-lo-dyen kak volk.
Я голоден как волк.

I'm starving!
ya u-mi-RA-yu s GO-lo-du.
Я умираю с голоду.

I can't think on an empty stomach.
ya nye mo-GU DU-mat na-to-SCHAK.
Я не могу думать **натощак**.

Do you have anything to nosh on?
YEST u te-BYA CHTO-ni-BUD po-KHA-vat?
Есть у тебя что-нибудь **похавать**?

Let's stop by a cafeteria.
da-VAi zai-DYOM v sto-LO-vu-yu.
Давай зайдём в столовую.
Usually Soviet style, very cheap, and reeking of *kotlety* (meat patties),
mashed potatoes, cabbage, and *kompot* (fruit juice).

Let's grab a snack!
da-VAI pye-rye-KU-sim!
Давай **перекусим**!

How much should we leave for **a tip?**
SKOL-ko o-STA-vit cha-ye-VIKH?
Сколько оставить **чаевых**?
It has become pretty common for Russian wait staff to expect a tip, no matter how lousy the service is.

Do they take **cards** here?
tut pri-ni-MA-yut krye-DIT-ki?
Тут принимают **кредитки**?

Bon appétit!
pri-YAT-no-vo a-ppye-TI-ta!
Приятного аппетита!

Let's get the food on the table.
da-VAI na-KRO-yem na stol.
Давай накроем на стол.

Help yourself! Don't be shy!
u-go-SCHAI-sya! nye styes-NYAI-sya!
Угощайся! Не стесняйся!

We have more than enough!
u nas vsye-VO KHVA-tit s go-lo-VOI!
У нас всего хватит с головой!

I prefer **home-cooked meals.**
ya pryed-po-chi-TA-yu do-MASH-nyu-yu KUKH-nyu.
Я предпочитаю **домашнюю кухню**.

I never say no to a chance to **chow for free.**
ya ni-kog-DA nye ot-KA-zi-va-yus ot SHAN-sa po-KUshat na kha-LYA-vu.
Я никогда не отказываюсь от шанса **покушать на халяву**.

My hotel offers a **buffet-style** breakfast.
mo-YA gos-TI-ni-tsa pryed-la-GA-yet SHVED-skii stol na ZAV-trak.
Моя гостиница предлагает **шведский стол** на завтрак.

That meat is **crazy expensive!**
E-to MYA-so STO-it BYE-she-ni-ye DYEN-gi!
Это мясо **стоит бешеные деньги**!

We've got a ton of **munchies** here.
u nas tut KHAV-chi-ka na-VA-lom.
У нас тут **хавчика** навалом.

I have a sweet tooth.
ya slad-ko-YEZH-ka.
Я сладкоежка.

I want a **cheese sandwich.**
ya kho-CHU bu-ter-BROD s SI-rom.
Я хочу **бутерброд** с сыром.
Buterbrody are open-faced sandwiches, so if you order a *buterbrod s sirom*, expect a slice of bread, a slab of butter, and a slice of cheese. American-style sandwiches are generally called сэндвичи (*SEND-vi-chi*).

I don't recommend the business lunch here.
BIZ-nyes lanch ne so-VYE-tu-yu zdyes.
Я не советую здесь пробовать бизнес ланч.

I could really go for some sushi.
MNYE by chut SU-shi.
Мне бы чуть суши.

Do you want a brownie or a muffin with your tea?
ty KHO-chesh BROW-ni i-LI MAF-fin k chai-YU?
Ты хочешь брауни или маффин к чаю?

Fast food
fast-FUD
Фаст-фуд

Holy shit, is American fast food spreading in Russia! You can find Papa John's, Sbarro, Domino's, Burger King, Cinnabon,

Subway, Carl's Jr., and of course, the granddaddy of 'em all, McDonald's. I think it's super lame to come halfway around the world just to eat the same over-processed crap you can eat back home, but sometimes, you just get a cravin'. When the Golden Arches call to you, what can you do but answer? Fortunately, if you know Cyrillic, the menus are pretty easy to decipher, and you probably have them memorized by now anyway. So here are just a few examples of the delectable fast food options that await you, should you find yourself down and out and hangry.

Let's go to McDonald's!
poi-DYOM v Mak-DO-nalds!
Пойдём в Макдоналдс!

That was one nasty hamburger!
E-to bil vo-ob-SCHE pro-TIV-nii GAM-bur-ger!
Это был вообще **противный** гамбургер!

Damn, I love fries!
blin, ya lyu-BLYU fri!
Блин, я люблю фри!

Could I get some ketchup?
MOZH-no chut KE-tchu-pa?
Можно чуть **кетчупа**?

I think I got food poisoning from that hot dog.
po-MO-ye-mu ya o-tra-VIL-sya E-tim khot-DO-gom.
По-моему я отравился этим **хот-догом**.

Let's grab some burritos at the food court.
da-VAI voz-MYOM bur-RI-to-sy na food-KURT.
Давай возьмём бурритосы на фуд-курте.

Can you get a decent pizza anywhere in Russia?
MOZH-no na-i-TI GDYE-ni-BUD v ro-SSII nor-MAL-nu-yu PITS-tsu?
Можно найти где-нибудь в России нормальную **пиццу**?

Do you know if that pizzeria **delivers**?
*nye ZNA-yesh, YEST li u E-toi pits-tse-RII **do-STAV-ka** na dom?*
Не знаешь, есть ли у этой пиццерии **доставка** на дом?

We have free delivery.
my do-sta-VLYA-yem byes-PLAT-no.
Мы доставляем бесплатно.

Let's order a pepperoni pizza.
da-VAI za-KA-zhem PITS-tsy pep-pe-RO-ni.
Давай закажем пиццу пепперони.

I'm going to get some chicken poppers at Papa John's.
ya voz-MU CHI-ken POP-pers u Papa Johns.
Я возьму чикен попперс у Папа Джонс.

Coffee break
pye-rye-RIV na KO-fye
Перерыв на кофе

Thank God for Старбакс (Starbucks), and there are now over 100 of them in Russia. No longer are the cold and thirsty denizens of Russia's major cities deprived of the simple joys of an overpriced cup of coffee served in one of three inscrutable sizes.

Give me, please....
DAI-tye po-ZHAL-uista....
Дайте, пожалуйста....

> **coffee**
> *ko-fe-YOK*
> кофеёк

fresh brew coffee
svye-zhe-za-VA-rye-nii KO-fye
свежезаваренный кофе

Arabica
KO-fye a-RA-bi-ka
кофе Арабика

espresso
es-PRES-so
эспрессо

French press coffee
KO-fye vo french-PRES-sye
кофе во френч-прессе

a tall pumpkin spice latte
TYK-vyen-no PRYA-nii LAT-te raz-MYE-ra TOLL
тыквенно-пряный латте размера толл

a grande cappuccino without sugar
ka-pu-CHI-no GRAN-de byez SA-kha-ra
капучино гранде без сахара

a venti caramel macchiato
ka-ra-MYEL ma-ki-A-to VEN-ti
карамель маккиато венти

a mocha Frappuccino
MO-ka fra-pu-CHI-no
мокка фраппучино

iced coffee
KO-fye sol-DOM
кофе со льдом

tea
chai-YOK
чаёк

a mango smoothie
MAN-go SMOO-zi
манго смузи

fresh squeezed juice
fryesh
фреш

That barista makes amazing latte art.
E-ta ba-RIS-ta DYE-la-yet u-di-VI-tyel-nii LAT-te art.
Эта бариста делает удивительный латте-арт.

....

I'm thirsty
mnye KHO-che-tsya pit
Мне хочется пить

I want to drink ...
kho-CHU po-PIT ...
Хочу попить ...
Note that this phrase is followed by the accusative.

> **some water**
> *vo-DICH-ku*
> водичку
> Be sure to stress this word right: *vo-DICH-ku*. If you stress it on the
> first syllable, it will sound like you are asking for some vodka.
>
> mineral water **on ice**
> *mi-nye-RAL-ku **so l-DOM***
> минералку **со льдом**
>
> **sparkling** mineral water
> *mi-nye-RAL-ku **s GA-zom***
> минералку **с газом**

Borzhomi

bor-ZHO-mi

Боржоми

A kind of salty-tasting mineral water produced in Georgia.

Narzan

nar-ZAN

Нарзан

Another popular kind of mineral water.

soda pop

ga-zi-ROV-ku

газировку

Gazirovka is short for газированная вода (*ga-zi-RO-va-nnaya vo-DA*). There is a Russian word сода (*SO-da*), but that refers to baking soda.

fruity soda

li-mo-NAD

лимонад

The confusion here is that Russian *limonad* usually has little to do with what English speakers call lemonade.

birch juice

bye-RYO-zo-vii sok

берёзовый сок

Who knew you could make juice from a tree?

Tarkhun

tar-KHUN

Тархун

This is a kind of green-colored soda made from tarragon and has been popular since Soviet times.

compote

kom-POT

компот

A kind of drink made from stewed fruit and sugar.

orange juice, **no ice**
*a-pyel-SI-no-vii sok **byez l-DA***
апельсиновый сок **без льда**

It's still pretty common for Russians to prefer drinks without ice in the belief that ice will cause sore throats. This is changing among the younger crowd, especially in urban areas, but elsewhere it persists.

kefir
kye-FIR
кефир

Apparently, this is very good for your digestive system.

sour milk
pro-sto-KVA-shu
простоквашу

kvass
kvas
квас

Nonalcoholic, carbonated, usually a little bitter, and popular in summer.

....

Yum yum
nyam nyam
Ням ням

I smell something **yummy.**
*ya SLI-shu O-chen **VKUS-nii** ZA-pakh.*
Я слышу очень **вкусный** запах.

That's a great **recipe!**
*E-to KLASS-nii **rye-TSEPT!***
Это классный **рецепт**!

What delicious food!
ka-KA-ya vku-SNYA-ti-na!
Какая вкуснятина!

Finger-lickin' good!
PAL-chi-ki ob-LI-zhesh!
Пальчики оближешь!

At the party there was a lot of **tasty food.**
na vye-che-RIN-kye BI-lo MNO-go VKUS-nyen-ko-vo.
На вечеринке было много **вкусненького**.

Russians love their food so, not surprisingly, they use a lot of diminutives when talking about it. While there is really no English equivalent that fully captures the meaning of most of these words, the diminutive endings convey a sense of affection, along the lines of saying "a nice little something or other." Here are few examples of the food that Russians love to show their love to:

Pass me some **nice little bread.**
pye-rye-DAI mnye KHLYE-bu-shek.
Передай мне **хлебушек**.

I'll have **teeny piece** of that **cakey.**
BU-du ku-SO-chek E-tovo TOR-ti-ka.
Буду **кусочек** этого **тортика**.

These **little salads** are very **yummy.**
E-ti sa-LA-ti-ki O-chen VKUS-nyen-ki-ye.
Эти **салатики** очень **вкусненькие**.

I really liked that **soupy-soup.**
mnye O-chen po-NRA-vil-sya E-tot SUP-chik.
Мне очень понравился этот **супчик**.

I love **sweeties!**
ya lyu-BLYU SLA-dyen-ko-ye!
Я люблю **сладенькое!**

Could you pass the **taters?**
pye-rye-DAI, po-ZHA-lui-sta, kar-TO-shech-ku.
Передай, пожалуйста, **картошечку.**

I adore pickled **'shrooms.**
ya o-bo-ZHA-yu -ma-ri-NO-va-nni-ye gri-BOCH-ki.
Я обожаю маринованные **грибочки.**

Give me a **little cookie**, I'm having a hangry attack.
dai mnye pye-CHYEN-ku—ya is-PI-ti-va-yu PRI-stup go-lo-ZLOS-ti.
Дай мне **печеньку**—я испитиваю приступ голозлости.

....

Yuck!
fuuuu!
Фуууу!

This **shit** reminds me of **prison swill!**
Et-o gov-NO na-po-mi-NA-yet mnye o ba-LAN-dye!
Это **говно** напоминает мне о **баланде!**

That's disgusting!
E-to pro-TIV-no!
Это противно!

That looks really **rank!**
E-to VI-glya-dit sov-SYEM khrye-NO-vo!
Это выглядит совсем **хреново!**

That yogurt is way **past its expiration date.**
E-tot YO-gurt dav-NO pro-SRO-che-nii.
Этот йогурт давно **просроченный.**

This slop is **inedible.**
*E-ta zhrat-VA **nye-sye-DOB-na.***
Эта жратва **несъедобна**.

I can't eat this **filth!**
*ya nye mo-GU yest E-tu **GA-dost!***
Я не могу есть эту **гадость**!

This grub **went bad** a long time ago.
*E-ta KHAV-ka dav-NO **pro-PA-la.***
Эта хавка давно **пропала**.

This fruit is already **spoiled.**
*E-ti FRUK-ti u-ZHE **is-POR-che-ni.***
Эти фрукты уже **испорчены**.

I **burned** the chicken.
*ya **pye-rye-ZHA-ril** KU-ri-tsu.*
Я **пережарил** курицу.

I'm afraid I **oversalted** the fish.
*bo-YUS, chto **pye-rye-so-LIL** RI-bu.*
Боюсь, что **пересолил** рыбу .

I've lost my appetite.
u me-NYA pro-PAL a-ppye-TIT.
У меня пропал аппетит.

I don't feel so well.
CHUST-vu-yu se-BYA nye O-chen.
Чувствую себя не очень.

That fish isn't sitting right.
E-ta RI-ba bi-LA nye-KSTA-ti.
Эта рыба была некстати.

I think I ate something bad.
po MO-ye-mu ya cyel CHTO-to nye TO.
По-моему я съел что-то не то.

That beef didn't go down right.
E-ta go-VYA-di-na po-PA-la nye v to GOR-lo.
Эта говядина попала не в то горло.

After trying Russian bread, I can never go back to that stale American crap.
PO-sle to-VO, kak PRO-bo-val RU-sskii khlyeb, BOL-she nye smo-GU KU-shat E-to nye-SVYE-zhe-ye ame-ri-KANsko-ye dyer-MO.
После того, как пробовал русский хлеб, больше не смогу кушать это **несвежее** американское дерьмо.

....

I'm full
ya sit
Я сыт

Refusing food in Russia is almost as hard as refusing a drink. In fact, most Russian hosts will force food on their guests with great passion and take it as a personal insult if you don't go for seconds or thirds. There is an unspoken rule in Russia when refusing food: The first time you refuse, no one will take you seriously. The second time, they still think you are being modest. Only after your third refusal will people start to get the hint that you've had enough.

I'm stuffed.
ya na-YEL-sya/na-YE-las.
Я наелся/наелась.

I'm gonna burst!
BOL-she nye mo-GU!
Больше не могу!

I've had enough.
ya u-ZHE VSYO.
Я уже всё.

I ate too much.
ya ob-YEL-sya.
Я объелся.

I overdid it.
ya pye-rye-bor-SCHIL.
Я переборщил.

It's time for a smoke break.
po-RA na pye-rye-KUR.
Пора на перекур.

....

Soups and salads
su-PI i sa-LA-ti
Супы и салаты

Borsht
borsht
Борщ
This is Ukrainian but is eaten widely in Russia. The main ingredient is beets, but it also usually has potatoes, carrots, cabbage, and sometimes meat. It's often eaten со сметаной (*so smye-TA-noi*)—with sour cream.

Ukha
u-KHA
Уха
A kind of fish stew.

Schi
schi
Щи
Cabbage soup

Solyanka
so-LYAN-ka
Солянка
A soup of vegetables and meat, usually a little spicy.

Kharcho
khar-CHO
Харчо
A spicy Georgian soup.

Okroshka
o-KROSH-ka
Окрошка
A cold soup usually served in summer, made of kvass, sour cream, radishes, green onion, cucumber, and sometimes potatoes and/or meat.

Vinegret
vi-nye-GRYET
Винегрет
A beet and vegetable salad.

Olivye
o-li-VYE
Оливье
Made of potatoes, egg, onion, mayonnaise, ham, and peas.

....

Meat
MYA-so
Мясо

Salo
SA-lo
Сало
Pig fat. Mmmmm! Perhaps more typical of Ukraine but eaten in Russia as well, particularly in villages.

Pelmeni
pyel-MYE-ni
Пельмени
Sort of like meat ravioli.

RUSSIAN FOOD
RU-SSKA-YA KUKH-NYA
РУССКАЯ КУХНЯ

The typical Russian meal usually comprises several courses, including soup, a main course, maybe a salad or two, and plenty of bread. After Russians finish eating, they often fire up the samovar and serve tea and coffee. You might already be familiar with some traditional Russian foods such as the tasty beet soup, borsht (*borsht*, Борщ). But it may take some convincing to try salo (*sa-lo*, сало), which is basically pure pig fat.

Cutlets
kot-LYE-ti
Котлеты

Roast
zhar-KO-ye
Жаркое

Congealed meat (or fish)
kho-lo-DYETS
Холодец

Herring salad
pod SHU-boi
Под шубой
This is like a big lump of fish salad covered with beets, eggs, potatoes, carrots, and mayonnaise.

Shashlik
shash-LIK
Шашлык
More than a food, this Caucasian version of the shish kabob brings with it a whole tradition of going out to the forest, building a fire, cooking up the marinated meat, washing it down with vodka, playing guitar, and having good, drunken fun.

Pierogies and blintzes
va-RYE-ni-ki i bli-NI
Вареники и блинчики

Vareniki...
va-RYE-ni-ki...
Вареники…
These are sort of like *pelmeni* but with different kinds of fillings. In the US, they are usually called pierogies. The most common kinds are:

> **with potato**
> *s kar-TOSH-koi*
> с картошкой

> **with cabbage**
> *s ka-PUS-toi*
> с капустой

> **with mushrooms**
> *s gri-BA-mi*
> с грибами

> **with cherries**
> *s VISH-nyei*
> с вишней

Blintz
bli-NI
Блины
Also sometimes called blini (блинчики/ *BLIN-chi-ki*), these are basically crepes that can be served with such things as:

> **with honey**
> *s MYO-dom*
> с мёдом

> **with sweet farmers cheese**
> *s TVO-ro-gom*
> с творогом

with sour cream
so smye-TA-noi
со сметаной

with caviar
s i-KROI
с икрой

with jam
s va-RYE-nyem
с вареньем

....

Bread
khlyeb
Хлеб

Black bread
CHOR-nii khlyeb
Чёрный хлеб

Small dried circles of bread
SUSH-ki
Сушки
Usually eaten with tea.

Gingerbread (sort of)
PRYA-ni-ki
Пряники
The taste is vaguely similar to gingerbread, but it most frequently comes
in either brick form or as cookies, which can be coated in powered sugar
or honey and are sometimes filled with sweet jelly.

Pirozhki
pi-rozh-KI
Пирожки
These are rolls filled with various things, most commonly potatoes,
cabbage, or meat.

Dessert
dye-SYERT
Десерт

Apple pie
YA-bloch-nii pi-ROG
Яблочный пирог
This is different from American apple pie. Instead of a crust with apple filling, it is more like a cake with apple chunks baked into the batter.

Napoleon
na-po-lye-ON
Наполеон
This is a pastry with layers of flaky phyllo dough slathered with rich cream.

Bird milk
PTI-chye mo-lo-KO
Птичье молоко
This is sort of like little square pieces of marshmallow dipped in chocolate, but not quite as sticky.

Ice cream
mo-RO-zhe-no-ye
Мороженое

Creamy kind of ice cream
plom-BIR
Пломбир

Ice cream bar
es-ki-MO
Эскимо

Acknowledgments

The authors would like to acknowledge the unrivaled magic of coffee, the cheesy goodness of quesadillas, and the adrenaline rush of a looming deadline.

About the Authors

Erin Coyne and **Igor Fisun** live in Northern California with their tween daughter and elderly Chihuahua. They watch way too much TV and should really try to get out more. When they're not glued to a screen, they enjoy traveling to Eastern Europe and pretending to be foodies.